Beautiful *for* Christ

O worship the Lord in the beauty of holiness

LaDwyina Tolar-Slater

ISBN 978-1-68570-075-1 (paperback)
ISBN 978-1-68570-076-8 (digital)

Copyright © 2023 by LaDwyina Tolar-Slater

All rights reserved. No part of this publication may be reproduced, distributed, or transmitted in any form or by any means, including photocopying, recording, or other electronic or mechanical methods without the prior written permission of the publisher. For permission requests, solicit the publisher via the address below.

Christian Faith Publishing
832 Park Avenue
Meadville, PA 16335
www.christianfaithpublishing.com

Unless otherwise indicated, scripture quotations are taken from the King James Version of the Holy Bible.

1. Walk with Christ; Christian women; religious life.
2. Christianity; religious teaching; beautiful spirit.
3. Worship in the beauty of holiness.
4. Put on spiritual fruit.

Cover Photo
"Celestial Cloudscape"
Located in the Orion Nebula
Photographed by the NASA/ESA Hubble Space Telescope. It captures the colorful luminous regions surrounding newborn stars.
Credits:
RELEASE: NASA/ESA
Permissions: Content Use Policy

Printed in the United States of America

This book belongs to

My Bonus Mom

Presented by

BRETT

Date

_9-14-2025_

In memory of my father, Joseph Walls Sr., and my daughter, LaDwyina Tolar-Bailey.

I dedicate *Beautiful for Christ* to God.

"O worship the Lord in the beauty of holiness:
Fear before him all the earth."
—Psalm 96:9

"Let the words of my mouth, and the meditation of my heart, be acceptable in thy sight, O Lord, my strength, and my redeemer."
—Psalm 19:14

Contents

Preface xi
Acknowledgments xv
Introduction xvii
My Prayer for You xix
Questions xxi
Part 1: God 1
          God and His Glory 3
          Salvation 8
          Baptism 12
          The Holy Spirit 16
Part 2: The Temple 21
          The Temple 23
          Trust 28
Part 3: The Holy Bible 31
          God's Positioning System 33
          The Holy Bible 35
          Study 40
          Internalization 44
          Wisdom 54
          The Ten Commandments 58
          Jesus's Commandments 59

	Love One Another 60
	God's Will 63
Part 4:	Prayer 65
	Prayer 67
	Different Types of Prayers 76
	Blessings 80
	Praise in the Beauty of Holiness 85
	Worship in the Beauty of Holiness 88
Part 5:	Fruit of the Spirit 93
	Fruit of the Spirit 95
	Love 96
	My Internalization of 1 Peter 4:13 100
	Joy 102
	Peace 105
	Long-Suffering 108
	Gentleness 113
	Goodness 117
	Faith 120
	Meekness 124
	Temperance 127
Part 6:	The Adversary, Satan 131
	Recognizing Satan 133
Part 7:	Beautiful for Christ 137
	Scriptural Procedures to Becoming Beautiful for Christ ... 139
	Walking in the Beauty of Holiness 142
	Allow Your Light to Shine 146
	Examine Yourself 149

Written Examination 153
Beautiful for Christ! 157

Preface

Beautiful for Christ was written to introduce the steps and processes of becoming beautiful for Jesus Christ while suggesting a technique to those that want to gain an in-depth understanding of God's Word by internalizing the scriptures. It has also been written for those that do not know how to become saved and for those that want to have a perpetuating relationship with God. *Beautiful for Christ* will explain how to accept Jesus Christ as your Lord and Savior to receive your salvation. It will also enlighten you on how to walk in the beauty of holiness, therefore giving you a relationship with God while allowing your light to shine. My inspiration for writing this book was a message from God given to me in a dream and inspired by God to write the vision and make it plain. *Beautiful for Christ* is written to inspire you to study God's Holy Word and to learn how to become Christlike with the spirit of love while worshipping the Lord in the beauty of holiness. Its purpose is to reveal to you how to become closer to God and to learn how to let your light shine by embracing the fruit of the Spirit that are the essence of Christ.

God's message came to me on a Saturday morning through a vision. There were three female choir members in my dream. We were in a circle, holding hands. As I prayed, the circle became larger with more women joining hands with us. I remember vividly seeing myself clothed in my white choir robe with tear-filled eyes while indwelled with the Holy Spirit, feeling the love and praises for God. It was a feeling of joy that nearly brought me to my knees. The experience in my vision is unforgettable. As I prayed in the circle, I cried tears of joy and praised God. The Holy Spirit instructed me to include the vision in *Beautiful for Christ* and that I should provide scriptures from the Holy Bible and instructions to enlighten others of God's glory and how to walk in the beauty of holiness to become beautiful for Christ.

After awaking, it was then that I realized that I had been given a message and that God had given me a vision and instructions on what I should include in this book. It was around 1:00 a.m. when the Holy Spirit instructed me to get a tablet and write. I kept thinking and telling myself that I would do it in the morning, but the Holy Spirit would not allow me to sleep. I continued to hear the message. I attempted to ignore the message for at least two hours, thinking that I would eventually return to my slumber. The Spirit continued to speak to me; I finally gave in to my instructions and began to write for several more hours until all the words were on paper. I wrote down the title and the chapters that were to be included in *Beautiful for Christ*.

I had not gone to bed thinking of authoring a book; however, God had a plan for me, and I am now following His will. I did return to sleep after writing everything down. When I awoke that morning, I knew that I had been called to help young ladies and women to find Christ and to help them become beautiful for Christ and to walk in the beauty of holiness.

I had a major operation and was home for several months, recuperating quietly. While recuperating, I spent most of my time reading the Bible and listening to a complete collection of the Holy Bible King James Version compact discs that my husband had given me. I used my Holy Bible to cross-reference what I was hearing to ensure what I was listening to was indeed the written Word inspired by God. I was totally absorbed and learned so much by listening to and reading God's Holy Word that I began to write and internalize scriptures. If I didn't understand the meaning of the scripture, I would ask my husband, Deacon Slater, the meaning, and I would read and listen to it again to get the correct understanding. The process of internalization became a natural procedure for me; I wanted complete and in-depth understanding of every word and the context in which it was used.

I continued to write when I received inspiration from the Holy Spirit. I found myself writing only when the Spirit gave me the words to put on the page. As I was writing one morning in the family room, I was sitting on the sofa, and my husband was sitting near me. The television was on a Gospel music channel.

While writing, I wanted to describe God's sunset, and I said aloud, "I wish I had a picture of a sunset so I could see all of the colors and how they blend and radiate." Immediately after saying that, I looked up from my laptop, and there on the television was a picture of a sunset. I told my husband who had just heard my request to look at the television.

When he looked, he saw the sunset and said, "God is working with you."

He asked if I thought I had been called. My response was yes, to write a book. I was so excited and amazed. I then shared with him the details of my dream that I have just shared with you.

I have heard people say the Holy Bible is hard to read and understand. *Beautiful for Christ* is also an introduction to the Holy Bible, showing you how to understand its compilation and to ensure you that you should not be intimidated by God's Word or how it is written. I believe practice makes perfect. In reference to reading the Bible, you can be rest assured that you will become comfortable with the art of the language used in the King James Version and realize that it is really beautiful. In my opinion, there is no book greater than the Holy Bible, and there are no replacements for it.

Acknowledgments

Thanks be to Almighty God for who He is and for all He has done.

Many thanks to Pastor Eugene Roberson and Pastor Dr. Fragier L. Funches, for your precious time extended in helping me to do God's will.

Thank you to my husband, Gregory, for spiritual support; my daughter Brittany for her technical support; my sisters Juanita, Evelyn, and Corrine for their encouraging words; and my niece Sidnice for her inspiration and fervent prayers. I love you.

Thank you to my publishing agent Brittney and the entire team at Christian Faith Publishing for believing in me.

Introduction

> I will take the cup of salvation, and call
> upon the name of the Lord.
> —Psalm 116:13

Because we live, we must drink from the cup of life and bear a cross. During our daily walk, we have a cup of life that is filled for us daily by God. This cup that has been handed to us also comes with a cross to bear. God will not give us more than what we can handle; however, it can become challenging as in the cross God gave to Jesus. God knew Jesus could bear it for all humanity—the cup of salvation.

Some events in life we do not expect or want; however, we must bear it if it is God's will. We must endure the bitterness with the sweetness. God has given us His Holy Word as a guide to carry us through our cup of life. Our cross to bear is all of our trials, tribulations, tests, and triumphs, but for this cup, God has also given us a sweetener to add to our cup so that life may be easier for us. This sweetener is His Son, Jesus Christ. God's love for His children is so strong that He sacrificed His only begotten Son to save us. Because Jesus loves us and is obedient to His Father God, Jesus drank from the cup of salvation and carried His cross so that we may have the gift of life.

The earth is God's creation—so large, magnificent, and self-sustaining. Always bright, the sun lights up the sky and warms our bodies, the waters quench our thirst, and the air is the continuous breath of life that fills our lungs. Leap into God's Holy Word, and know you have moved from the darkness of the world into the brightness of light. How can we recognize beauty in darkness? We must have light to know, see, and feel God's beauty and glory, then we can become a light—the lamp that illuminates brightly to show the world the beauty and glory of God.

Accept Jesus as your Lord and Savior, abide by God's will, and learn and commit to His Holy Word and doctrine, understanding and internalizing the scriptures that God has given you for guidance and accepting what He has planned for you. By doing so, your light will shine, and God will recognize your beauty of holiness, then you will begin your journey to become beautiful for Christ. There is so much to read, understand, and internalize in God's Holy Word.

Spiritual growth is a process that everyone must go through when you have God in your life. There is a reason for our lives here on earth; many of us may not know what our purpose is or how to find it. The brief time that we spend walking here on earth should be cherished and nurtured by everyone who has received His beautiful gift of life.

Go along with me by reading *Beautiful for Christ*, giving your undivided attention to God's Word, growing in faith and prayer while discovering your purpose here on earth: learning how to let your light shine. Having faith in God and His will is very important in your growth while asking and allowing God to reveal to you your true purpose. By submitting to God's will, you will learn to pray, ask for forgiveness, guidance, and listen when God speaks to you. Your life will blossom more beautifully than you can imagine. You are like a diamond in the rough being cut and polished to full beauty and brilliance. Your increase will be more than you have room for, and you will then be able to bless others with your beautiful love for God. Jesus will recognize you and open a line of communication through Him to His Father God in heaven, and your soul, heart, and mind will be opened to receive God's everlasting love while becoming beautiful for Christ.

My Prayer for You

Heavenly Father, I boldly approach Your throne of grace and mercy with a bowed-down head and humbled heart, asking that You give Your mercy, guidance, wisdom, knowledge, and understanding of Your Holy Word to the readers of *Beautiful for Christ*. Lord, You said in your Holy Word in Matthew 7:7: "Ask, and it shall be given unto you; seek and ye shall find; knock, and it shall be opened unto you." Father God, I am asking that You touch each and every reader, doer, and hearer of your Holy Word, blessing each of them in a mighty way and showing them great favor. For this is my payer, in Jesus's name I pray. Amen.

Questions

B elow are questions that you will find the answers to as you read *Beautiful for Christ*.

Who is God, and what is His glory?
What is salvation, and how do I receive it?
Why should I become baptized?
What does baptism symbolize?
What are the essence of your soul?
What is the temple?
Who is the Comforter?
What are the spiritual gifts?
What are the fruit of the Spirit?
Why should I internalize?
How do I internalize?
Why should I become beautiful for Christ?

PART 1

GOD

God and His Glory

I am Alpha and Omega, the beginning and the
ending saith the Lord which is and which was,
and which is to come, the Almighty.
—Revelation 1:8

And one cried unto another, and said, Holy, holy, holy,
is the Lord of Host: the whole earth is full of his glory.
—Isaiah 6:3

The glory of the Lord shall endure for ever:
the Lord shall rejoice in his works.
—Psalm 104:31

Who is God? "In the beginning was the Word, and the Word was with God, and the Word was God" (John 1:1). God is the Trinity. The one true God the Father; the Holy Spirit; and the Son of God Jesus Christ, are collectively one supernatural spiritual Being (John 10:30). Almighty God is the Creator of heaven, earth, and all that is within and upon it. God's glory is the essence of Himself and all His works. When we say "Glory, hallelujah to God," we are acknowledging, as we believe, it is to be the highest praise to God and that the glory of God is His power and might described as the following: omnipotent (almighty, all powerful); omnipresent (present everywhere at all times), omniscient (all knowing); salvific (our Savior); holy (divine), magnificent; brilliant; radiant; gracious; merciful; miraculous; peaceful; loving; truthful; joyous; long-suffering; gentle; good; faithful; temperate; meek; He is Life and Resurrection.

What is God's glory? God's glory is the distinguished qualities that only He possesses and all that are within Him including the products of His works. God's glory is His Son, Jesus Christ, born of the Virgin Mary who came down from heaven to do God's will. God is bigger than what we Christians think or know of Him. God is Alpha and Omega. What is Alpha and Omega? God is the beginning of all existence, the presence of His Spirit before creation, and the ending at His will when He says it is so Revelation 1:8. Because of His mystery, we are told to lean not unto our own understanding; God is I AM, and His glory will endure forever.

God is energy, the atom, nucleus, protons, neutrons, and electrons. He is the Creator of gravity, axis, and rotation; He is the ray of the sun that the eyes should not look upon and the light of the moon that glows at night, and He is the twinkle in the stars. God is the Creator of the atmosphere, planets, nebula, and all galaxies in space. Astronomers believe that they are discovering new planets and stars that have spontaneously formed. Because of my belief, I know that God is alive; He is creating new planets and stars. God represents the elements: the air that was breathed into Adam's nostrils, the fire that revealed Himself to Moses as I AM in the un-consuming burning bush, the water that was made still in the presence of His disciples, and the earth that was created from void. God is time, controlling a moment in the twinkling of an eye and transfiguration. With God's control of rotation, we have the seasons: winter, spring, summer, and fall. God is here with us now in the present; He is all around us and in everything, seen and unseen. God is the essence in everything that is good, perfect, and pure. God has protected His works with mysteries to show that He is God and that no man can be compared to Him or duplicate His creations. Has man duplicated the galaxies, stars, moon, or the sun?

Jean-Baptiste Lamarck proposed the first theory of evolution, which was his explanation of the existence of man followed by publication in 1858 by Charles Darwin and Alfred Russel Wallace. I am fast-forwarding to make a long story short with Charles Darwin becoming the father of evolution. I have heard what the professors have said, and I have refused to internalize their theory. In addition to evolution, physicists have come up with the big bang theory. I have heard that as well, and I am standing strong with the Word of God. Without God, there were no planets, and without planets, a big bang cannot occur. To read that Darwin is the father of evolution or his testimony on how man came to this earth is strange and unacceptable since Charles Darwin is not the Creator. Their theories are dependent upon God's creation already in existence. Man is still trying to understand the mighty works of God. It will forever be a mystery; God has hidden the answers and put the world in the heart of man.

>He hath made every thing beautiful in his time: also he hath set the world in their heart, so that no man can find out the work that God maketh from the beginning to the end. (Ecclesiastes 3:11)

>The Heavens declare the glory of God; and the firmament showeth his handiwork. (Psalm 19:1)

I have a friend, Luevera, whom I attended high school with. She texted me a picture of her interpretation of God's glory; it was beautiful. The picture captured the scene of rippling waters, green trees with the beautiful blue sky above—a very picturesque view of God's glory. She sent a group text that said, "I challenge you all to take one picture showing God's beauty and share it." Luevera asked for a picture of God's glory. I texted her two pictures; the first picture was of a hot-pink peonies in full bloom with bright golden-yellow centers. The second picture was of the sky, ocean, and waves beating against the shores and rocks breaking into splash droplets and sprinkling the vegetation, sustaining its life; it was a picture of God's glory at work. The water's colors in the photo are a reflection of the sky so brilliant with the same vivid color of indigo blue in the deep water, and the crashing of the waves against the rocky shores reflected the whiteness of the small puffs of clouds that were in the sky with the sun brightly shining. Those two pictures captured what I believed to be reflections of God's glory.

This was a group text. Our other friend Susan also sent her interpretation of God's glory, and she captured the sun rising above the horizon glowing like a silent alarm waking up the earth, with different shades of gold and yellow. As I studied the picture, I was able to see the shades change from the strongest boldest golden yellow to the brightest yellow at the height of the sunrise. The brightness captured in the picture was like the brightest sunlight that drivers try to avoid in the morning while driving to work. It was like an alarm clock saying, "Wake up, world. Drink from the cup of life, and see what God has planned for you." The pictures were all beautiful and spectacular representations of God's glory.

I mentioned earlier how I wanted to see God's sunrise, and surprisingly, the picture appeared on the television. I have since received a picture of God's sunset that was taken in Nicaragua and sent to me by my daughter Julene. The beauty that was captured was an artistic masterpiece of blended colors. The upper left of the picture is the sky that has hues of peach, coral, and pink with splashes of yellow blended throughout. This view was obstructed by the fronds of the palm tree silhouette. As I inspected the upper-right section of the picture, I noticed the indigo sky was very vivid in the background with the silhouette of a double palm beautifully hanging down from the tree. Beneath the palm, the colors of the sky had changed to pink, sky blue, peach, and orange. As I panned down beneath the coconuts hanging from the tree I saw the brightest yellow imaginable surrounded by a palette of all the mentioned colors blended softly into the horizon.

The sunset is a breathtaking masterpiece. Only God can create a painting of that magnitude in the sky without a paintbrush, paint, or watercolors while using the sky as the canvas. What artists can you name that has painted the sky? I smile as I type the answer. The name of the artist is God Almighty.

Luevera sent another picture of God's glory. The text said, "God's kiss." I looked at the picture, and with my eyes, not using my imagination, I did see God's kiss. I did clearly see the indigo-blue sky with one cloud in the center of the picture. The cloud she captured was in the form of a pair of lips puckered with a kiss angled down to all that love Him. How amazing is that?

The clouds are God's glory, and they will form at His will. I say glory, hallelujah to You, O Lord. "Holy, holy, holy is the Lord of Host: the whole earth is full of His glory" (Isaiah 6:3).

Salvation

Salvation belongeth unto the Lord: thy
blessing is upon thy people. Selah.

—Psalm 3:8

Neither is there salvation in any other: for
there is none other name under heaven given
among men, whereby we must be saved.

—Acts 4:12

That if thou shalt confess with thy mouth the Lord
Jesus, and shalt believe in thine heart that God hath
raised him from the dead thou shalt be saved.

—Romans 10:9

Our soul and salvation are one of the most profound and precious gifts that God has blessed us with. When God breathed into the nostrils of Adam the breath of life, he received a living soul. God has blessed everyone with a soul; the essence of our soul are our mind and heart. God has gifted us with the ability to use our mind with thought and reasoning that gives us free will—the ability to make decisions. God has also given us an innate emotion of love within our heart, and our soul is blessed with the beautiful essence of love needed to please God. Because we were born into sin, God has given us salvation, the way to eternal life, by the stripes of Jesus. Our soul is redeemed from the consequences of sin. Because it was God's will, Jesus Christ gave His life for us. "There is none other name under heaven given among men, whereby we must be saved" (Acts 4:12). We cannot buy salvation or receive it from any other being because salvation belongs to God (Psalm 3:8).

To receive salvation, you must confess. You may be wondering by now what are you going to confess and how you should confess to God. Most people may believe that confession is admitting to a sin committed, which is true albeit there is also a positive definition of confession. I would like to bring to light the positive meaning of confession in your life. Take a moment and consider what a positive confession may mean. You can confess to performing a good deed if someone has asked. You can also confess your love for someone. Positive confession can be known as verbally making known something that is of good nature. Now that I have brought to light that you can confess the good as well as the bad. I must inform you that confessing your faith has nothing to do with any sins or good deeds committed. To confess can also be defined as to declare faith by admitting openly to profess freely your religious belief. By the confession of your faith in Jesus Christ and believing in your heart that God has raised Jesus from the dead, you are securing your salvation (Romans 10:9–11).

Ephesians 2:8–9 says, "For by grace are ye saved through faith; and that not of yourselves: it is the gift of God: not of works, lest any man should boast." Can you imagine the economics of supply and demand of salvation? May I present to you a couple of horrific hypothetical scenarios? Salvation is needed to get into the kingdom of heaven, and you are one of the many that do not have salvation in the last day before the trumpet sounds. You assumed that you could buy salvation, but you did not have enough cash on hand because the price of salvation has skyrocketed. To make the scenario even worse, the banks and ATMs are closed; they no longer exist; only the extremely wealthy with huge amounts of cash on hand will be able to afford it, causing many people around the world to become priced out of God's gift. What would you do? Or can you imagine the many works that people have done while bragging that their works are more pleasing to God than yours or mine, they also are believing that God will give them entrance into heaven before you or me? I raised those two scenarios, hoping to get you to think about the fact that we do not know when our time will come, and if you have not accepted Christ, you are taking a chance of losing your soul. I thank God that I do not have to worry about my salvation because I have accepted Jesus Christ as my Lord and Savior, and I do believe He is seated at the right hand of our Father God in heaven (Hebrews 10:12).

I am also blessed in knowing that salvation is a gift from God (Ephesians 2:8).

You must not be afraid nor ashamed to confess your faith in God, which may be witnessed by the congregation, your family and friends. You are professing that you have accepted Jesus Christ as your Lord and Savior; however, you may accept Him at any time, even in private. You should give Christ the same type of love that He gives you. Agape is the type of love that Jesus has given and continues give us—His brotherly love of affection and protection. If I were given a choice to denounce Jesus to live, I would choose to die, showing my affection and knowing that I am returning the same agape love to Him; however, Jesus does not expect us to die for Him. Salvation is made of love and eternal life.

Next, you must repent, walk away from sin, and pray, asking God for forgiveness. Jesus mentioned *repent* more than one hundred times in the Bible, indicating that it is very important that you repent properly to gain forgiveness for your sins. Repentance is a serious and intentional turnaround or change in your life involving your behavior, speech, actions, reactions, and thoughts. You must humble yourself, feeling it in your heart, mind, and soul and giving all reverence to God while asking for forgiveness. Just think of it as spring-cleaning of your heart, mind, and soul. Examine yourself, think back over your life, and bring forward to your memory any and every sin that you may have committed knowing that it was not acceptable in God's sight. Ask God to forgive you by naming each sin that you committed. Promise God and yourself that you will not sin in that manner again. You must become aware of everything you think, say, and do. Internalize your promise, and commit it to memory and actions. Your promise is your bond with God. Much more than an agreement with a handshake, He expects you to keep your promise.

You cannot bargain with God. You can only make a promise to God. Because we are born sinners, we will sin again. We are not perfect; only God is perfect and pure. For that reason, we must always ask God for forgiveness and repent. This does not give you a pass to continue to repeat the same sin because you believe that God will forgive you. By reading God's Word, you will gain wisdom; and with wisdom, pray and ask for understanding. I will also speak repetitiously as Jesus did in regard to repentance. I will continue reminding you to seek the Holy Spirit to ask for wisdom and understanding.

Once you have received understanding and are aware that you are sinning, do you believe God will be happy with you if you continue to repeat the same sins? The answer is no, and for that reason, it is important that you allow God's will to be done in your life. When God is involved in all that you do or say, your deeds will be acceptable in His sight. Hebrews 10:26 says, "For if we sin willfully after that we have received the knowledge of the truth, there remaineth no more sacrifice for sins." The meaning of the above scripture must be internalized for the protection of your salvation.

It is important to have a pastor, a man of God, to guide and teach you the Word of God as you grow in faith while trusting in the Lord. You will also need a place to worship and a private area in your home to worship. Select a church that believes in God the Father in heaven, Jesus Christ the Son, and the Holy Spirit. You may have to visit several churches to find the one that you trust and are comfortable with.

Romans 10:13–14 says, "For whosoever shall call upon the name of the Lord shall be saved. How then shall they call on Him whom they have not believed? And how shall they believe in Him of whom they have not heard? And how shall they hear without a preacher?" The church that you join should have Sunday school and Bible study classes to help you learn God's Word. You must hear, read, and study the Bible and internalize. Once you have accepted Jesus Christ, become a candidate for baptism to become born again.

Baptism

There is one Body, and one Spirit, even as ye are
called in one hope of your calling; one Lord, one
faith, one baptism, one God and Father of all, who
is above all, and through all, and in you all.
—Ephesians 4:4–6

And Jesus, when He was baptized, went up
straightway out of the water: and, lo, the heavens
were opened unto him, and he saw the Spirit of God
descending like a dove, and lighting upon him.
—Matthew 3:16

Therefore we are buried with him by baptism
into death: that like as Christ was raised up
from the dead by the glory of the Father,
even so we also should walk in newness of life.
—Romans 6:4

Nicodemus asked Jesus in John 3:4, "How can a man be born when he is old? Can he enter the second time into his mother's womb, and be born?" Christ explained that unless man is born of the water and Spirit, he cannot enter God's kingdom (John 3:5). Before baptism, you must humble yourself before God. Repent by making a change, turning away from sin, praying, and confessing your sins, then ask God to forgive you; you will be forgiven and cleansed (1 John 1:9).

Baptism is one of the most important ordinances, an authoritative decree, from Jesus. After the confession of your faith in Jesus Christ, you can become a candidate for baptism, which is the immersion of your entire body into the water to symbolize the death and burial of Christ, and upon lifting you out of the water, the resurrection of Christ is symbolized in preparation for your walk with Christ (Romans 6:4).

Jesus was baptized by John the Baptist and immersed in the Jordan River; when Jesus came up out of the water, a dove, symbolizing the Holy Spirit, landed on his shoulder, and a voice from heaven, being God's voice, was saying that Jesus is His Son and He is well pleased (Matthew 3:16–17). You will become baptized in the name of the Father and of the Son and of the Holy Ghost, collectively called the Trinity of God. We want God to be pleased with us; therefore, we must become baptized to become Christlike, walking in the newness of life. Upon baptism, you are considered born again, and according to the Scripture, you will receive the gift of the Holy Ghost, your newness of life, which is the Holy Spirit within you.

After you have been baptized, you are a newly reborn person. Pray for wisdom and understanding, then begin your walk, honoring God. Because we are born in sin, we must continually repent and ask for God's forgiveness. If any person believes that he or she is not a sinner, they are only deceiving themselves. For example, to tell a lie is the spirit of Satan who is the father of all lies because he does not have the truth within him (John 8:44).

> For all have sinned and come short of the glory of God. (Romans 3:23)

We must diligently work toward becoming beautiful for Christ; this is one of your Christian duties. I say one because you will accept many duties during your walks with God; the Holy Spirit will show you what your calling is in your Christian journey. You must increase your faith by asking God to allow the Holy Ghost's presence to shine brighter within you and His voice to become louder within your subconsciousness and consciousness so that you may clearly hear

His pure counsel speaking to you and guiding you to do God's will. Learn to listen, feel, and recognize the Holy Spirit moving within you to provide you with wisdom, understanding, and knowledge.

John 14:26 says, "But the Comforter, which is the Holy Ghost, whom the Father will send in my name He shall teach you all things, and bring all things to your remembrance, whatsoever I have said unto you." The Comforter came to me and brought both scriptures to my conscious memory and carried me through the hardest time in my life and continues to carry me and give me strength. The Comforter will also carry you if you believe.

The following are several of the spiritual gifts that the Holy Ghost will provide to you: wisdom, understanding, counsel, fortitude, knowledge, piety, peace, and fear of the Lord.

Fearing the Lord is the beginning of wisdom, and wisdom is the natural ability to exercise reasonable decisions from knowledge gained through experience and knowing God. Praying, defining, internalizing, and studying the Scriptures will help you understand what you are reading. By listening to your inner spirit, your Holy Ghost's counsel will guide you to behave within the fruit of the Spirit. The utilization of your spiritual gifts will allow your light to shine for all to see. Fortitude is the strength of your mind and body to resist the wiles of the world and to stay focused on God and endure your cup of life as Jesus did. Knowledge is your awareness that you are following the will of God and His commandments. Piety is your devotion, faith, and your dutifulness to God. Fearing the Lord is the utmost respect for God in all that you say and do. All spiritual gifts are blessings from God provided by the Comforter.

Second Corinthians 5:17 says, "Therefore if any man be in Christ he is a new creature: old things are passed away; behold all things are become new."

You now have a new life that needs to be nourished with God's Holy Word and cultivated by faith to grow into beauty while preparing for your walk with Christ.

Your mind, your soul, and your heart should always remain on the Lord. Do not look back onto the life of the world. Look forward to be rewarded in life here on earth with God's favor and in spirit; your reward is the kingdom of heaven.

You have a new life, a new desire with the understanding of your reward: eternal life with God. Cherish your new walk in life, and let no one take it away from you.

Your church may require you to attend Bible study classes and Sunday school. Upon completion of required classes, you will have gained a new family with the same interest, your new brothers and sisters in Christ. After receiving the right hand of fellowship, which is a welcoming ceremony given by some churches, you will have the opportunity to consider joining one or more of the ministries in the church, such as the choir, usher board, or praise dance ministry. Your new family will welcome you with open arms. The ministry you join should have regular meetings and rehearsals. Your duty as a member is a serious commitment to the auxiliary with the mission of honoring God.

Because we are humans and imperfect, there may be some people who will judge you or your past. Rest assured that God has already forgiven you, and know that there is no one that you will come into contact with that is without sin, for we all have sinned. So remain focused on God, not on hearsay or gossip.

Romans 3:24–25 says, "Being justified freely by his grace through the redemption that is in Christ Jesus: Whom God hath set forth to be a propitiation through faith in his blood, to declare his righteousness for the remission of sins that are past, through the forbearance of God." All praises to Almighty God. You have been redeemed because Jesus paid the price of your past sins; thereby, you have been forgiven by the mercy of God. Glory, hallelujah to you, O Lord.

The Holy Spirit

> Then Peter said unto them, repent,
> and be baptized every one of you in the name
> of Jesus Christ for the remission of sins,
> and ye shall receive the gift of the Holy Ghost.
> —Acts 2:38

> But the Comforter, which is the Holy Ghost,
> whom the Father will send in my name, he shall
> teach you all things, and bring all things to your
> remembrance, whatsoever I have said unto you.
> —John 14:26

> But when the Comforter is come, whom I will send
> unto you from the Father, even the Spirit of truth, which
> proceedeth from the Father, he shall testify of me.
> —John 15:26

Who is the Holy Spirit? The Holy Spirit is the Spirit of God, the divine essence of God that moved upon the face of the waters when the earth was empty and without form (Genesis 1:2). God was speaking to the supernatural members of His Holy Trinity when He said, "Let us make man in our own image, after our likeness" (Genesis 1:26). The Holy Spirit is one of the spiritual Beings within the Holy Trinity. The proof can be found when Jesus asked God to send the Comforter (the Holy Spirit) to be with us while He is away to bring truth from God testifying of Jesus (John 15:26). In that scripture, you will find Jesus, God, and the Comforter mentioned in the same verse, and they are the Trinity.

While Jesus is in heaven, the Comforter speaks to us. He is our Connection to God and our Messenger that gives us good and pure thoughts and answers from God. One of the most significant responsibilities of the Holy Spirit is to interpret the Holy Scripture, the Word of God, for our understanding. The Comforter is our Helper, our Counselor, and Guidance of pure Spirit. The Holy Spirit is here and living within the people that believe in God the Father, Jesus the son of God, the Holy Spirit and has been baptized in the spirit. The presence of the Holy Spirit is a powerful indwelling within your temple. He speaks to your consciousness and subconsciousness.

The Holy Spirit is able to move within you if you allow yourself to listen when He speaks and are obedient to His good and pure counsel. The Holy Spirit is also Might, Counsel, Wisdom, Understanding, Knowledge, Fear of the Lord (Isaiah 11:2), Truth (John 14:17), Life (Romans 8:2), Revelation (Ephesians 1:17, and Prophecy or the Testimony of Jesus (Revelation 19:10). All of those spiritual gifts, the Holy Spirit will give to you upon your asking. To receive your spiritual gifts, you must become humble, obedient, and dependent upon God's Holy Spirit and sensitive to listening and becoming obedient when He speaks to you. Have you ever received God's grace? The answer to that question is yes. When Jesus Christ asked God to send the Comforter, you were provided grace with unmerited divine assistance from the Holy Spirit for your regeneration or your spiritual renewal.

Christ knew that we would need guidance while He was away also because of His agape love graced with mercy. Jesus asked God to send the Comforter. Have you ever tried to understand the meaning of a scripture but continued to be unsure, not completely comprehending the true meaning until understanding was turned on like a light bulb? It was the Holy Spirit revealing it to you—an act of divine communication. If you are impatient, I ask that you have patience. The Spirit is going to reveal to you the meaning of God's marvelous scriptures and bless you with wisdom and understanding. Have you ever looked for an object in a dark room but was unable to locate it until the light was turned on? The Holy Spirit turns on that light for you, allowing you to understand the messages from God.

The Holy Spirit is our Interpreter that will reveal the meaning of God's Holy Word. The object that was not seen is an example of our incomplete understanding of the Holy Word without the help of the Holy Spirit. Can you imagine what the Holy Spirit can and will do for you if you ask? According to Scripture, the Comforter will teach us all things heard from God and will remind us of all things learned and stored away; hence, one of the reasons why studying God's Word and retaining it is extremely important. It can be called up, brought back to your memory, and utilized when needed. By the grace of Jesus, He did not leave us comfortless. The Holy Spirit will provide us with good pure directions, instructions, information, and answers from God. The Holy Spirit will also bless you with all the gifted attributes if you prepare yourself and allow the Spirit to shine within you. Ask in Jesus's name, and you shall receive the many comforts and spiritual gifts the Holy Spirit has in store for you.

In the past, I wondered how I would feel when filled with the Holy Spirit. I have learned that everyone's experience of the Holy Spirit's indwelling is different by observing and speaking with others. When the Holy Spirit is moving within me, my arrector pili muscles contract, causing the hair on my arms and the back of my neck to stand up straight. I feel a cool light covering fall upon me like a soft sheer veil floating slowly down from heaven, covering me so lightly while surrounding me completely, as if God has surrounded me with His loving arms. I am totally aware when this happens, and I can feel the indwelling within me as I pray, praise, and worship God. I feel as though the Spirit is letting me know that God is with me, and He is pleased. It is a feeling that I will welcome, cherish, and remember forever.

The Holy Spirit speaks to me when it is decision time; the Spirit is clear in guiding me to the correct decisions to be made. If I do not listen in reality, I have decided to become disobedient by not doing God's will. I feel as if I am in a state of conviction, and I immediately realize it falling upon me. I must admit, I rather walk in the light than deal with conviction. The Comforter has provided me all that Jesus has promised. I have been given wisdom, understanding, prophecy, revelation, and the fear of God.

Listen to your inner spirit of goodness and light. If the message is of peace, love, truth, harmony, goodness, meekness, gentleness, forgiveness, long-suffering, hope, and faith in God, you are hearing from the Holy Spirit. Know that if there are thoughts that are not pure and good, they are not from God. I thank God for answering my prayers and for blessing me with the Holy Spirit and my spiritual gifts.

Christ has promised that He will never leave us comfortless (John 14:18). The Holy Spirit will reside with us while Christ is away. "But the Comforter, which is the Holy Ghost, whom the Father will send in my name, He shall teach you all things, and bring all things to your remembrance, whatsoever I have said unto you" (John 14:26). For that reason, you must study and retain the Word of God. No one can take God's Scripture away from you. The Holy Spirit will remind you of God's Holy Word in your times of need.

The darkest time in my life was the death of my daughter LaDwyina. I received the heartbreaking phone call in the middle of the night, awakening me from my sleep. My daughter Brittany called to tell me her sister LaDwyina had died. The pain and shock that Brittany was feeling, I felt immediately when I heard her voice delivering the bad news to me. Brittany's pain became my pain, in addition to my own. I felt the pain of Brittany's loss of her big sister. While growing up as children and as adults, they talked together, laughed together, shared secrets, and fussed as siblings do. I also felt the pain of her having to give me the sad and painful news. I ended the call and called LaDwyina's husband. I was told that she did not make it. I didn't understand; I asked her husband, "Did not make what?" His response was: "She had died." I did not have a chance to fully comprehend the news, and I had so many questions, but I clearly heard the voice of the Holy Spirit, the Comforter, speaking to me, saying: "Trust in the Lord with all thine heart" (Proverbs 3:5–6).

I recognized the Holy Spirit speaking to me. I responded in my mind, "Yes, Lord, I will trust You." I also heard the Spirit say, "She is not dead but sleepeth" (Luke 8:52). I heard those words, and peace and strength took control of my emotions and actions. I didn't have time to cry. I had business to take care of for LaDwyina's funeral. There were no tears at that time; I was walking in the Spirit with the strength of God.

I began to find things to do around the house to keep busy for hours as people came over to the house. I remained busy until the Holy Spirit told me that it was time to go to Savannah. I did exactly as I was told. Now when I find myself thinking about LaDwyina, I cry privately to hide my many burning tears of pain and loss. I have never felt tears like this before. It feels as though a harmful chemical is in my eyes, causing them to burn. When this happens, immediately the Holy Spirit reminds me that she is only sleeping, then I feel peace fall upon me again. I have pictures of LaDwyina in her casket; I sometimes look at them and can see that she is sleeping. Can you imagine how God may have felt knowing the pain His Son, Jesus, endured on the cross while Christ was still living, hanging until He gave up the Ghost? I to this day continue to dry my tears and find peace because I hear the Comforter and recognize His voice.

I have received inspiration and messages from the Holy Spirit while writing *Beautiful for Christ*. The Holy Spirit would speak to me during my quiet and private moments of the early mornings before dawn or late nights before I fall asleep. I remember awakening very early one morning while lying in bed. I opened my eyes and saw a white cursive script sentence floating slowly in the air above my bed for me to read. I stared at the sentence and read it. I did not have any other thoughts except that it was a message from the Holy Spirit. I was told to include a section regarding the Holy Spirit in *Beautiful for Christ*. I immediately recognized that the Holy Spirit was speaking to me because the message was good and pure. The Spirit has been guiding me as I write, and I thank God for the presence of the Comforter. I immediately went to my laptop and added the Holy Spirit to the table of contents and began reading God's Holy Word.

PART 2

THE TEMPLE

The Temple

> What? Know ye not that your body is the temple
> of the Holy Ghost (which is) in you, which
> ye have of God, and ye are not your own?
> For ye are bought with a price: therefore glorify God
> in your body and in your spirit, which are God's.
> —1 Corinthians 6:19–20

> I beseech you therefore, brethren, by the mercies
> of God, that ye present your bodies a living
> sacrifice, holy, acceptable unto God, which is your
> reasonable service. And be not conformed to this
> world but be ye transformed by the renewing of
> your mind, that ye may prove what is the good,
> and acceptable, and perfect, will of God.
> —Romans 12:1–2

After praying and asking the Holy Spirit to reveal to me the meaning of God's Word and committing to intense study and understanding, I have learned that the Temple in heaven is God, Jesus, and the Holy Spirit. In the book of Revelation 21:22, it says, "And I saw no temple therein: for the Lord God Almighty and the Lamb are the Temple of it." I asked myself, how large is heaven? The answer that the Holy Spirit has given me is that heaven does not have boundaries or boarders; it is a space that cannot be measured by man. God and the Lamb, Jesus, is the Temple of it. Now ask yourself, how large is the Temple? The answer is: God is immeasurable. I made that point to say that this reminds me that I am made in God's image; therefore, I am the temple, the embodiment of my soul and spirit that must be kept holy to glorify God. However, our temple can be measured because we are humans and our bodies are not immortal. Our temple is infinitesimal in comparison to the temple of God. I ask then, why is it so difficult for most people to maintain their temple for the Holy Spirit? If we truly believe, we should be able to keep our temple immaculate.

In the book of 1 Corinthians 6:19–20, the scripture says, "What? Know ye not that your body is the temple of the Holy Ghost which is in you, which ye have of God, ye are not your own? For ye are bought with a price: Therefore glorify God in your body, and in your spirit, which are God's." I repeat, glorify God in your body. Now ask yourself, what does that mean? It is important for you to know and always remember that your body is the temple for the Holy Ghost. You are to respect your temple and glorify God in it. Respecting your temple is a combination of knowing God's Word and walking in the beauty of holiness. I am not writing to judge anyone; that is for God to do. I also know that no one is perfect; however, you should continue to try to keep your temple holy.

If your temple, your body, is full of profanities, alcohol, cigarettes, drugs, lies, and everything that Satan stands for, do you believe the Holy Ghost would want to dwell within? You being the temple are bigger than worldly pleasures. It is the vessel that God has given you that the Holy Spirit may reside within.

Repenting and turning away from the wiles of the world can consecrate your temple, ridding it of what is not acceptable in God's sight. Dedicate your heart to God, commit to getting wisdom and understanding of what you are asking God for; and pray fervently, asking God for strength, knowledge, and endurance for the purification of your temple, which will allow the Holy Spirit to dwell within a beautiful temple while also actively becoming closer to God with fasting, praying, praising, worshipping, and reading God's Holy Word with unbreakable commitment.

The Holy Bible speaks of marking your body in Leviticus 19:28: "Ye shall not make any cuttings in your flesh for the dead nor print any marks upon you: I am Lord."

God has made you in His image. He is perfect, and there is no need for changes because you are perfect in God's sight. Jesus kept His temple holy and without defilement. If you choose to mark or tattoo your body, know that you are going against the will of God. Because you have free will to make your own decisions, may I suggest that you refrain from using the mark of the beast? You may ask, "What actions may defile the body?" That would be anything that goes against or contrary to sound doctrine of God and the teachings of Jesus.

First Corinthians 3:17 says, "If any man defile the temple of God, him shall God destroy, for the temple of God is holy, which temple ye are."

What does it mean to present oneself as a living sacrifice to God? God no longer expects or require us to give burnt offerings as a sacrifice to Him. You are the temples of the Holy Ghost, and all that you think and do must be with a clean loving heart, with the Word of God in your spirit, because you are holy while giving up anything that is against God's doctrine. That is not too much to ask of us. God is not asking for us to give the lives of our children as a human sacrifice to Him. He is asking those that love Him to use their temple as a living sacrifice by turning away from worldly ways and to live holy. We must refuse to fill our temples with addictive drugs, alcohol in access to drunkenness, overeating to harm your health, or excessive smoking. Those are some of the vices that can harm your temple and should be given up. This is not written to judge you; it is written so that you may judge yourselves.

I have come in contact with people that have informed me that they do not eat pork because it is bad for them; however, he or she may drink copious amounts of alcohol until they become inebriated or use drugs until they are in a state of being unaware of their surroundings. I have heard people say in defense of their drinking, "Jesus turned water into wine, and drinking is not bad for you." Drinking is bad for you if you drink into drunkenness or alcoholism. Yes, Jesus did turn water into wine for a wedding celebration, and the Scripture also says, "Be sober, be vigilant; because your adversary the Devil, as a roaring lion, walketh about, seeking whom he may devour" (1 Peter 5:8). We all know vices are and can be addictive habits that are harmful to the body (your temple) and may cause an accelerated death. I cannot count the number of times that I have heard in the news about an innocent person killed in a car accident by someone driving under the influence of alcohol or mind-altering drugs. The Holy Ghost wants to dwell in a pure and holy temple, and God will help to free anyone of his or her vices if He is asked in prayer in the name of Jesus.

An important step to becoming beautiful for Christ is taking care of God's temple. If you love Him, you will love His temple also; to love His temple is to follow God's will by presenting our bodies as a living sacrifice using God's Word to care for yourself spiritually as well as physically. God has asked us to give up and sacrifice the desires of our heart that are not good for our heart, mind, and soul.

Doctors suggest at least eight hours of sleep per night and drinking plenty of water while eating fruits and vegetables daily and exercising. As we know, no one is perfect although we try and try again to follow the medical advice. I ask you why many of us are not aware of what God wants for our bodies? The closer you are to God, the more you will pull away from the world. As you distance yourself from living in the world, you will also distance yourself from chances of other worldly sins, such as profane language, fornication, adultery, lying, murder, etc. We are born into sin because Adam and Eve disobeyed God; however, because our eyes are opened, we now know the wiles of the world.

I have two concerns, and I cannot continue writing unless the following topics are mentioned: your speech and attire. Your speech will give a signal to others regarding your true inward spirit of your heart and mind. Be careful of what you say to ensure that your light shines for Christ. Our speech is a reflection of what we are thinking and feeling. James 3:6 says, "And the tongue is a fire, a world of iniquity: so is the tongue among our members that it defileth the whole body, and setteth on fire the course of nature; and it is set on fire of hell." Disparaging comments directed toward someone may inflict emotional pain that cannot be retracted from the mind of the receiver once the remarks are heard. It is evident in social media the damage that is caused by the tongue or by the stroke of a key. If you have hurt someone because you did not control your tongue, you should ask for forgiveness from God and from the person that was hurt. Conversations or oral exchanges that we have should be swift to listen to, slow to speak, and slow to anger (James 1:19). Proverbs 16:24 says, "Pleasant words are as an honeycomb, sweet to the soul, and health to the bones." Also, God does not want us to swear by oath (James 5:12).

My second concern is attire. I am not suggesting that you make yourselves look any less than what God has blessed you with. Nor am I suggesting that you purchase new clothing because God will accept you as you are; however, I would like to remind you that Jesus was a modest man that could have worn the finest of clothing. He knew that His outward adorning was not His purpose for being here on earth. You are the salt of the earth, possessing savor, and are of greater value to God than the clothing you wear. Concentrate on becoming one with the fruit of the Spirit by dressing yourself spiritually and allowing your spirit to become more prominent than the clothing you wear. Your purpose is for the glory of God. Your outer attire as well as your spirit reflect your respect that you have for God.

As you grow closer to God, you will have a better understanding and desire to care for your temple. It will be a challenge because the adversary, Satan, wants you to fail. Pray and ask God for strength and guidance, and listen to your Holy Spirit. He will guide you. Whatever you do in word or deed, think of Jesus, and ask yourself, are you doing it in His name? If your deed is not in His name, then listen to your Holy Spirit and stand, be still, and do not act. Wait on the Lord to guide you with His will.

Trust

Trust in the Lord with all thine heart; and lean not unto thine own understanding. In all thy ways acknowledge him, and he shall direct thy paths.
—Proverbs 3:5–6

O taste and see that the Lord is good: blessed is the man that trusteth in him.
—Psalm 34:8

Commit thy way unto the Lord; trust also in him; and he shall bring it to pass.
—Psalm 37:5

In the previous section regarding the Holy Spirit, I spoke to you about the darkest time in my life. I am bringing the passing of my daughter to your attention again because I also know that my trust in God and the Holy Spirit was the major factor that allowed me to hear the soft whispers and to listen as the Spirit spoke to me. I trusted the message that I received from the Holy Spirit and also understood that God had sent the Comforter to me because Jesus said, "I will not leave you comfortless: I will come to you" (John 14:18). My family and friends wondered how I was able to function as I did; my answer to everyone is it was by the grace of God that I received my strength. I trusted in the Lord with all of my heart, and I did not question God. God directed my path to Savannah, Georgia, and comforted me.

Regarding trust, have you ever had an acquaintance or friend tell you that they heard about a diet and suggested that you try it? After trying the diet, you later realized it was a fad and not healthy for you. Or have you purchased gadgets, believing that because it was advertised on television, it was great and would make life easier in the kitchen, only discovering that when you attempted to use the gadget, you could have finished the dish much sooner and easier without it because you had not considered the learning curve? You believed and had faith that the gadget was a great idea. Before global positioning systems and cellular phones were invented, had you ever pulled into a gas station for directions? After following the directions of the attendant, you realized that the person either did not truly know how to direct you to your destination or that they intentionally sent you in the wrong direction.

I bring up those scenarios to make the point that you trusted a stranger and acted upon their recommendations. At that time, your trust was 100 percent, or you would not have asked or tried whatever it was that was presented or suggested to you. This is the type of trust that you need when you accept Jesus Christ as your Lord and Savior 100 percent. There is no room for doubt. Can anyone tell you that Jesus guided him or her in the wrong direction or told him or her to hate? I can tell you, the answer is no. God is good and pure all the time; He does not deceive you nor tempt you. He is the same today, as He was yesterday and forevermore (Hebrews 13:8). Trust in the Lord. He will show you the lightened path that you should take. Allow Him to lead and guide you.

Trust and faith are sometimes used synonymously. Imagine when a person goes to the doctor seeking medical treatment for an illness. He or she will choose a particular physician because they trust the recommendations received, and the doctor's credentials appear to be perfect, causing him or her to make the decision to allow the doctor to give treatment or perform a procedure. It is the trust and faith that caused them to believe the doctor is excellent and the prognosis will be a full and successful recovery.

I sometimes wonder why so many people do not have that same faith and trust in God as they do in consumer products that are sold before FDA approval, as in trial drugs. For instance, vitamin supplements that have not been approved by the FDA make claims of cures and treatments for different medical conditions such as weight loss pills for the morbidly obese, weight-gain supplements for malnourished, and hair-growth serums for thinning hair, just to name a few. I must admit, I also trusted unapproved supplements; I was very thin as a young adult and wanted to gain weight. To make a long story short, the weight-gain chews did not work. I gained weight naturally over time after giving birth to four children, and now I am praying to lose weight. I know. Go figure that one out.

Yet we still believe in men and their medical creations until it backfires and is brought to light and revealed by breaking news the harm it will cause if consumed. Have you ever heard of God backfiring in your face? I don't believe anyone has. God is love, and all goodness comes from Him. Jesus will never ask you to do anything wrong nor tempt you in anything against God's will.

Why then is it a problem to have faith and trust in God? No one can prove any wrongdoings by God. People should think in a positive manner, saying as my pastor would say, "It is better to have God and not need Him than to need God and not have Him." By trusting in the Lord, you will be blessed (Psalm 34:8).

Look back over your life, and think about your experiences. Are you able to say that life was great and you could have not done anything differently? Or does your examination of yourself tell you that had you known God, you would definitely have asked God to guide you and let His will be done? It is never too late, as long as you have breath in your body, to trust God and do His will. Commit yourself to God, and "He shall bring it to pass" (Psalm 37:5).

PART 3

THE HOLY BIBLE

God's Positioning System

> I will instruct thee and teach thee in the way
> which thou shalt go: I will guide thee
> with mine eye.
> —Psalm 32:8

> And I will bring the blind by a way that they knew not; I will lead them in paths that they have not known: I will make darkness light before them, and crooked things straight. These things will I do unto them, and not forsake them.
> —Isaiah 42:16

In today's society, Global Positioning Systems (GPS) are found in many motor vehicles and are also applications for cellular phones. The GPS is used to help us navigate our way from point A to point B or to our final destination. By programming into the GPS information regarding your starting point and the address to your final destination, this will give you directions. It will also give information to the highways or roads that should be taken and the amount of time it will take to arrive. The GPS will inform you if there is an accident ahead and if there is police waiting for speeding cars. Many people around the world use and trust the directions of this electronic device and may even swear by it. I know of a written GPS that has been around since Moses. I believe men and women depend too greatly on the electronic GPS; therefore, I would like to introduce you to the original GPS. However, I need to reassign the meaning of the acronym to *God's Positioning System*.

Look to the greatest book ever written which can be found in most bookstores around the world and online. My personal preference is the King James Version. The title of God's positioning system is the Word, the Holy Bible. In it you will find that God created the heaven and the earth and that Jesus Christ teaches us by speaking in parables and by giving a beautiful sermon on the mountain. Before you begin reading, pray and ask the Holy Spirit to give you wisdom and understanding of God's Holy Word.

The Holy Bible

All scripture is given by inspiration of God and is
profitable for doctrine, for reproof, for correction, for
instruction in righteousness. That the man of God may
be perfect, thoroughly furnished unto all good works.
—2 Timothy 3:16–17

For whatsoever things were written aforetime were
written for our learning, that we through patience
and comfort of the scriptures might have hope.
—Romans 15:4

Inspired by God, the Holy Bible was written so that we may have hope while in earthly life and eternal life to come. Have you heard that history repeats itself? Scripture says, "There is nothing new under the sun" (Ecclesiastes 1:9). That scripture reminds me of another scripture, Psalm 91:3, which says, "Surely he shall deliver thee from the snare of the fowler, and from the noisome pestilence." The *snare* is the asymptomatic trap, the *fowler* is the hunter named COVID-19, *noisome* is the offensive symptom affecting the senses, especially your sense of smell, and *pestilence* is the contagious disease. Virulent is the rapid and destructive course taken upon the people all over the world; that is, the pandemic. Isn't that amazing? The current pandemic that the world is trying to overcome, the Bible has already spoken of it. Psalm 91:4 says, "He shall cover thee with his feathers, and under his wings shalt thou trust: His truth shall be thy shield and buckler." God will shield and protect everyone that put his or her trust in Him. If you have faith in God, you will have faith in the knowledge that He has given the scientists to protect you from covid and all its variants.

The Holy Bible was written for correction so that we may learn and have understanding of the past to better prepare us to become righteous and perfect in the present and future for God. I ask that you explore for yourself the Holy Bible and find that it was written so that we may have hope in the future by learning from the past. "For whatsoever things were written aforetime were written for our learning" (Romans 15:4). Some people may never read the entire Holy Bible, and some may never pick it up; however, to learn God's doctrine and gain wisdom and understanding, you must read and study God's Holy Word. By reading the Bible, you will learn that "the man of God may be perfect and thoroughly furnished unto all good works" (2 Timothy 3:17).

The Bible will start with the first book, Genesis. In it, the Trinity is creating heaven and earth. Moving forward, Moses was called into a personal and revealing relationship with God on Mount Sinai, where he received the Ten Commandments. You will learn more about Moses as you read; however, I spoke of Moses because he is credited with writing the first five books of the Holy Bible that was inspired by God. I will present to you scriptures from the Holy Bible to assist you with locating God's words that will explain to you how to become saved and enlighten you to the scriptures that will inspire you to continue to study and show yourself approved. You will also have to abide by God's Ten Commandments, which can be found in the book of Exodus 20. Please read the chapter in its entirety and also the last verse of Deuteronomy 5:33.

If the Bible is new to you, please acquaint yourself with it. Find where the New Testament begins, and commit yourself to learning the compilation of the books starting with Matthew and ending with Revelation, the last book of the Bible. As mentioned previously, you may require help in understanding God's Holy Word; you must pray, and you will also need to hear the Word of God from a preacher whom has been called by God to preach it.

Now that you know God, you must pray, praise, respect, and acknowledge Him in all that you do and constantly ask God to reveal His will and allow His will to be done in your life. In the Bible, you will find that God has given us the book of Proverbs as a guide that should be followed by all who want to walk in the light.

I ask that you give your studies your undivided attention, and if the Holy Bible is read faithfully and His commandments are followed religiously, you will receive knowledge and wisdom while moving toward God's plan for you. You may wonder how you should approach reading the Bible. May I suggest that you take a few moments to acquaint yourself with your Bible? Upon examination, you may find, located in the front, that there are some suggested approaches to reading it. In my personal Bible, I found that there are several choices on how to approach the goal of reading the Bible by following the suggested tracks.

The first track is an introduction to the Holy Bible, taking a total commitment time of six weeks by reading the suggested books and chapters on the teachings of Jesus, continued by reading about the life and teachings of Paul, and ending the first track reading in the Old Testament. The second track method suggests that the reader can read every book in the Bible starting with Genesis and ending with Revelation. The commitment time is approximately six months. The third and final track suggested reading every word of the Bible with the commitment time of approximately three years. I personally chose the first track that starts with Luke chapter 1 and ends with Jonah chapter 1.

I would like to also mention that each track outlined the chapters that should be read for completion of that particular track; you may also notice in the mentioned first track that I chose the books and chapters from were not read consecutively.

Let's learn the names of the books as they are categorized. If you start with the first book, the book of Genesis, and count the books forward, you will be able to learn the names of each group of books as they are categorized. For example, Genesis, Exodus, Leviticus, Numbers, and Deuteronomy are the five books of the law inspired by God and written by Moses, followed by the next twelve books: Joshua, Judges, Ruth, 1 Samuel, 2 Samuel, 1 Kings, 2 Kings, 1 Chronicles, 2 Chronicles, Ezra, Nehemiah, and Esther. These are the books of history. This same method can be used for the book categories in the New Testament starting with Matthew, Mark, Luke, and John. These four are the books of the Gospel.

With close examination, you will learn about the contents of the Holy Bible. There are sixty-six books in the Bible that are divided into two main divisions, the Old Testament and the New Testament. These two divisions are further divided according to writings.

The first thirty-nine books of the Bible are found in the Old Testament that is divided as such.

The first five books are called the books of law, followed by twelve books of history, five books of poetry, five books of major prophets, and twelve books of minor prophets. The last twenty-seven books of the Bible are called the New Testament, which is divided in this way: the first four books are called the Gospel, followed by one book of history, fourteen letters, seven general books, and ending with the book of prophecy. Wow, that is amazing. The Holy Bible is inspired by God. No wonder it's the most-read book in the world. You must study and learn God's Word, and the navigation of the Bible will come to you naturally over time.

I hope you are as excited as I am because God and His Holy Word is your GPS for life! Read it, study it, internalize it, believe it, and practice God's doctrine.

The Bible is your guide; it can direct you to the path, leading you to become blessed with eternal life. It will also guide you to the correct road to take when you stray, hit bumps in the road, come to low valleys of sadness, or have hills to climb the normal struggles of life. God's comforting words will reassure you, when you read, that He will never leave you.

The Bible will guide you when you turn onto a one-way street believing that hard times will never end and you cannot turn around. It will give you direction when the road is too steep and you need that push of inspiration by believing that you can do all things through Christ who gives you strength. It will guide you when you're lost or reach a dead end. By reading the Bible and paying close attention to the spoken words of Jesus in the New Testament, you will become refreshed and strengthened. Remember, God knows all. He will pick you up when and if you should fall. He knows the map of your life, the roads you should take, and the roadblocks that you will encounter if you should stray.

Study

Of these things put them in remembrance, charging them before the Lord that they strive not about words to no profit but to the subverting of the hearers. Study to show thyself approved unto God, a workman that needeth not to be ashamed, rightly dividing the word of truth.
—2 Timothy 2:14–15

And that ye study to quiet, and to do your own business, and to work with your own hands as we commanded you.
—1 Thessalonians 4:11

When you study according to scripture, you are asked to put the scripture into remembrance to internalize and show yourself approved (2 Timothy 2:14–15). I remember being a babe in Christ standing in church on a Sunday morning, and my pastor would say, "Open your Bible to a particular book and scripture." I would try to find it as fast as possible, but by the time I located the scripture, the responsive reading would be over or nearly over. Then I learned to glance around me to determine the direction the other members of the congregation were turning their Bible pages to. If they opened their Bible toward the front, I would look toward the front, and if they opened their Bible toward the back, I would start looking in the New Testament. I did not want to immediately look in the table of contents because I was ashamed, and I did not want those seated near me to know that I was not able to navigate the Bible. I also found out by following in the same direction of the other members that they did not always navigate in the right direction, moving from the front of the book to the back then to the front again or vice versa. To my surprise, I was not alone; they also needed to learn the compilation of the books in the Bible.

I felt as though I was very slow in locating requested scriptures, and I believed that everyone seated near me knew that I did not know how to navigate the Bible. I was determined to learn, and I committed to memory and learned that if I opened the Bible in the middle, the pages will be near the books of Proverbs and Psalms. Then I learned that the book that precedes Psalm is the book of Job and the book that came after Proverbs is Ecclesiastes. To study means to make serious efforts to reading and attempting to understand, then you will show yourself approved when you have learned to quiet and do your own business according to scripture (1 Thessalonians 4:11).

Before you begin reading, pray and ask the Holy Spirit to give you understanding of God's Holy Word. The more you read and understand, the greater is your wisdom. The Holy Spirit is wise and will give counsel to those who will listen, and if you have questions, the answers will be revealed to you. You may also ask your pastor to explain; however, to learn, you must read and study to also understand the sacrifices that God and Jesus made for us and to know what is expected of us in return. The Bible will explain everything you need to know and believe to be saved and have everlasting life. Then you will not question if you are saved; you will know that you are saved and born again.

I have presented and will present to you scriptures from the Bible to assist you with locating God's words that will show you how to become saved and scriptures that will inspire you to continue to study and show yourself approved by becoming beautiful for Christ.

As you study the Holy Bible, you will read in the Old Testament about the prophet Isaiah who predicted the coming of Jesus more than seven hundred years before His birth, the reason for His coming, and the manner of death. You will also learn in the New Testament about the birth of Christ, His teachings, and the fulfillment of the scripture prophesied by the prophet Isaiah: the death of Christ. You will also learn how to pray in the manner in which Jesus instructs us to pray (Matthew 6:6–8). Also in Matthew 6:9–13, Jesus gives us the perfect words to pray, also known as the Lord's Prayer, albeit some may call or refer to it as the Disciple's Prayer.

This is only the beginning. You will have copious amounts of information to digest, learn, and understand as I also continue to learn God's Holy Word with you. As you become closer to God, may I suggest that you attend Bible study and Sunday school classes? This will help you ask and receive answers to the questions you may have. This is when your light will begin to shine as you practice and internalize God's Holy Word. Most importantly, give your studies your undivided attention as you work toward your reward: the kingdom of heaven.

Who is without sin? The first thought that comes to my mind is a babe; however, this cannot be true because we are born into sin. Jesus died for our sins; however, God did not want us to commit sin unknowingly. Therefore, He informed us of the sins that we are asked not to commit through the Ten Commandments. God knows all. He sees and hears everything we are doing and thinking.

I have heard mentioned that we do not have to abide by the Ten Commandments because we are under the law of the land and bound by the New Testament. To my understanding, that is not entirely true. The law of the land binds us in society, and God's law in the Old Testament binds us to God's will. "Jesus is the same yesterday, and today, and forever" (Hebrews 13:8). Jesus would never go against God's will because Christ and God are one. Jesus gave us commandments that we must follow also in the New Testament. I do believe that love covers all of the commandments. If we love God, we will not elevate any person above Him nor make any graven images to worship or go against His will. If we love God, we will not use His name in vain. We should only call His name with reverence and seriousness, not using His name as a figure of speech. You should call on God when you want to praise Him or give a testimony about His goodness and mercy. Call on God in prayer, worship, or to thank Him.

We must obey all of the commandments with love for everyone in our hearts because love conquers all sin (1 Peter 4:8). Therefore, we should continue to recognize God's original law in addition to the laws in the New Testament given by Christ and the laws of the land (Romans 13:1–7).

Internalization

Internalization, according to *Merriam-Webster*, is defined as: "to incorporate (values, patterns of culture, etc.) within the self as conscious or subconscious guiding principles through learning or socialization." Scriptural internalization of the Holy Word is a process of reading, understanding, believing, accepting, incorporating, and actively practicing God's doctrine within self as conscious and subconscious principles. Before internalizing, pray and ask God to allow the Holy Spirit to reveal to you the meaning of the scriptures, then begin reading, isolating, and defining every unknown word as you read while getting wisdom and understanding. Commit the meaning of the scriptures to memory and into your heart. Before you quote or recite a scripture to someone, ensure that you understand and have internalized the meaning; you should feel and believe it in your heart. I have internalized the Lord's Prayer. When I pray, I grasp every word when it is spoken aloud or silently, believing, understanding, and feeling it in my heart. When you practice internalization, you will be enlightened and discover the true messages that God is revealing to you.

Take time to read your favorite scriptures. Internalize them to become enlightened, then store them in your heart and mind, allowing the scripture to become a part of your subconsciousness and consciousness by incorporating and practicing what you have learned in all your walks in life. To get the correct meaning of a scripture, may I suggest that you read the chapter or book in its entirety? Think of the lack of understanding you may have.

If you arrived at the theater in the middle of a movie, play, or opera, you may not completely understand what is happening or what roles the characters are playing. The same is possible with reading only a portion of a chapter or one scripture of a book in the Bible. Sometimes you may have to read the scripture more than once, and that's okay because you just want to understand its true meaning.

During your studies in high school, you may have been taught about medieval times, the history of the Middle Ages. Try to recall information about the times between the thirteenth and sixteenth centuries when the knights would compete by jousting and engaging in a fight on horseback by charging and pointing a lance forward toward their opponents in hopes of knocking one another off of their horses. The lance was made of the strongest hardwood possible, and the tip of the lance was made of iron or steel for penetration or piercing the armor the knights wore. Before jousting, the knights would prepare themselves by putting on their heavy protective suit of armor covering their heads and leaving openings for their eyes. They would also cover their chests, legs, hands, and feet.

I have spoken of the knights to inform you that you will have to do the same as them. Prepare yourself by putting on your spiritual full armor of God in preparation for battle against whatever evil may come to try to break your faith and trust in God. As the lance was to the knights, their weapon, so as the Holy Bible is to you. It is your weapon—your sword—the Word of God. Hebrews 4:12 says, "For the word of God is quick, and powerful, and sharper than any two-edged sword, piercing even to the dividing asunder of soul and spirit, and of the joints and marrow, and is a discerner of the thoughts and intents of the heart." God cannot be deceived; He is omniscient. If you are a babe in Christ, it can be easy for you to return to old habits of the world. You must not give in to those who want you to continue in the ways that you have turned away from. If that means you must not speak to or hold company with old acquaintances that are of the world, so be it. Hold on to God's unchanging hands. He is a friend that will not let you down.

I ask that you take time to pray and ask the Holy Ghost to reveal to you the meaning of the following scripture and that you internalize the meaning and follow the directions that are given to you.

> Wherefore take unto you the whole armour of God that ye may be able to withstand in the evil day, and having done all, to stand. Stand therefore, having your loins girt about with truth, and having on the breastplate of righteousness; And your feet shod with the preparation of the gospel of peace; above all, taking the shield of faith, wherewith ye shall be able to quench all the fiery darts of the wicked. And take the helmet of salvation, and the sword of the Spirit, which is the word of God: Praying always with all prayer and supplication in the Spirit, and watching thereunto with all perseverance and supplication for all saints. (Ephesians 6:13–18)

I speak of symbolism in my internalization interpretations of the full armor of God. By no means should the term *symbolism* be taken lightly because in reality, the full armor is the essences of Jesus Christ.

My interpretation of the full armor of God is saying to me, "Put on the essence of Jesus Christ." The armor in the scripture are the symbolisms of the Spirit in Jesus, all He stands for, and His commitment to the fulfillment of the Holy Scripture and God's will. Imagine Jesus on the cross, and visualize His full armor that He wore in His Spirit in life and in death on Golgotha Hill.

Jesus's outer garments were stripped from His physical body before hanging Him on the cross, revealing parts of his human anatomy. Starting with His loin's girt with the truth, the cloth that Jesus wore to Calvary wrapped around His loins represented His belt of truth. "Jesus is the way the truth and the life" (John 14:6).

Christ's natural breastplate, His torso, was bare, revealing His muscles. Jesus's actual breastplate of righteousness was uncovered for everyone to see; Jesus had nothing to hide. A breastplate of armor that was worn in those times was shaped to resemble the human anatomy by forming it to accommodate and protect the muscles. The righteousness on the inside of Jesus's breastplate tells it all. His precious spirit of divine morality, truth, respect, and His marvelous mercy, is that not the meaning of righteousness? Think of Christ hanging there; visualize His righteousness within.

Jesus's feet were shod as He went about His Father's business starting at the age of twelve and continuing throughout His life while learning, teaching, and preaching the Gospel of peace. Although His sandals may have been simple in fashion, Christ's feet were covered, shod by the Holy Spirit in all His walks here on earth. No man can fill the grand sandals of Christ. They nailed His feet to the cross, hoping to prevent Christ from coming down, thereby, in their minds, preventing Him from moving and performing miracles and teaching. No one can prevent the teaching of the Gospel. God's disciples, His children, you and I, are all over the world today spreading the Gospel of peace.

Visualize His arms stretched out wide, straining to contract every fiber of his muscles to take the weight away from his palms that were nailed to the cross with no relief from the weight of Christ's body and gravity pulling and tearing His palms. In one hand, He is holding the shield of faith. You may be thinking now that Jesus was not holding a shield. The scripture says in Hebrews 11:1, "Now faith is the substance of things hoped for, the evidence of things not seen." You do not visually see the shield of faith nor any of the other armor because faith is not by sight; however, Jesus showed us His faith by doing God's will after praying in the garden of Gethsemane. We know His faith is there because of the Scripture. Jesus had so much more faith than the size of a mustard seed because Christ believed in His heart that if His temple was destroyed, He would raise it up in three days (John 2:19). Can you imagine how many mustard seeds it would take to become the amount of faith that Jesus possesses? The great faith that Jesus has in His Father is unimaginable and incalculable nor can it be put into visual terms in regard to size. I can only say, "Thank You, Jesus, for having great faith."

In Christ's other hand is the sword, the Holy Bible, the mighty Word of God. For symbolism's sake, visualize a sword standing on its tip with the (grip) handle at the top, and beneath it, the (cross guard) causing the sword to resemble a cross when standing on its tip and vice versa; the cross resembles a sword. Jesus was crucified on the cross because the mighty Word of God had to be fulfilled. Jesus was standing on the Word of God with His arms outstretched to God like the cross guard of a sword. Jesus said, "It is finished He bowed His head and gave up the Ghost" (John 19:30). Jesus paid the price for our salvation. His job here on earth was finished. He died so that we may live; Jesus completed the will of God. When I read the Holy Bible, I remind myself that it is my sword. The Word of God contains everything we need to know, and it teaches us that God will fight our battles.

Deuteronomy 20:4 says, "For the Lord your God is he that goeth with you, to fight for you against your enemies, to save you." When I think of the helmet of salvation, I imagine a crown made of sharp thorns that was pressed into the head of Christ, piercing His flesh and causing His precious blood to stream down His face. Christ suffered so that we may live.

The full armor represents the essence of Jesus, and God has instructed us to put on the Spirit of Christ. If your walk is with God, your entire being and soul will have His protection. He has given us the instructions in the Scripture on how we should prepare ourselves for our journey with Him and for protection from the adversary in the evil day. God protected Job; He did not allow Satan to touch Job's soul. Think of your protection of salvation, and understand that God will not allow Satan to touch your soul when your mind and heart are synchronized with God and walking in the Spirit.

We must remain truthful, our *loins girt about with truth*, protecting our inner spirit from the beginning of understanding God's holy words in all aspects of life—truthful with God, our marriage, parenting, work, teachings, and with one another until the trumpet sounds so that we may live. John 14:6 says, "Jesus saith unto him, I am the way, the truth, and the life: no man cometh unto the Father, but by me."

If we cannot be truthful, how can we walk with Christ in the beauty of holiness? Some may believe that telling a small lie or a white lie to keep from hurting someone is okay. The truth of the matter is lies do not have color; however, if someone chooses to believe so, no matter what color that is assigned to, the lie, it remains a sin; and all sin carry the same weight as any other sin. God is the Judge to determine our sins, and it is God that will give us pardon and forgiveness. We must internalize and practice truthfulness to be Christlike. Jesus is Truth. To walk with Him, you must become like Jesus, and to walk with His light, you must also shine, mirroring His light, the brightest light imaginable. Jesus will not change His ways to conform to us. He expects us to change our worldly ways and become like Him.

The *breastplate of righteousness* is your badge of honor and a visible announcing of your integrity through your works and daily actions, showing that you are pressing forward, following all laws of religion which is divine law, and striving to follow the laws of the land which is moral law. Your breastplate of righteousness brings you closer to Christ, and your actions will inform your acquaintances that you cannot be swayed into wrongdoings; your righteous walk in the light will become an example for others and may turn those that are lost in the world toward God because they can see your love and respect for God, your self-respect, and the respect for others.

Righteous is what God asked us to become. Becoming morally good, following all of God's commandments and laws, is what God expects from us. The breastplate symbolizes our morals, character, virtue, probity of integrity, which collectively help to protect us from the darts of the adversary, keeping evil from penetrating our heart and love for God.

Having your *feet shod* is to turn toward God in the Gospel with peace in your heart and in all of your walks of life while preparing to understand and practice God's doctrine. There are many decisions to be made throughout life, and if you ask God to order your steps, to lead and guide you, He will show you the way where you should go. When you ask God to have His way, the steps that you take will be covered, shod spiritually. The steps will be with Christ in peace, love, and forgiveness as you go through your cup of life. God will light the path and send you in the direction of His essence: the fruit of the Spirit.

Having your feet shod is allowing God to work miraculously in your life, guiding your steps. By walking with Christ, you will walk away from conflict and sin to the path of peace, pressing toward the Gospel. Having your feet shod is like having sturdy, equipped boots on with a strong foothold dug into the side of a mountain like a climber headed to the summit of Mt. Everest with no turning back. While following the light of God, there is no slipping without getting up and trying again as you mature and become beautiful for Christ. Obstacles will appear. You have to listen to your Comforter and react in the way Jesus would.

My daughter Brittany and I were driving one early evening down Jackson Street. A car of angry young men pulled up on the left side us and told us to move over, get out of the way. I found the request to be strange because there were only two lanes, and we were in the right lane, and the men were in the left lane. They were yelling and cursing. While that was happening, the Spirit told me to turn right at the next street to avoid any further contact with them at the light. I followed my Spirit and turned. It was a very frightening moment, but I listened and obeyed the Holy Spirit. He guided us to safety, toward the Gospel of peace.

The *shield of faith* symbolizes your faith in God, the same faith in God that Jesus has shown to us when He carried His cross to Calvary, believing that He will have eternal life upon completing God's will by drinking from the cup that He asked God to take away from Him if it is God's will. No matter what battles or storms may come your way, you must believe that God will handle everything for you. No matter how down you may feel, you must have faith that God will pull you through the storm, and you must believe that He will turn your darkest night into a beautiful day if you keep the faith.

Having faith the size of a mustard seed will allow you to go through your daily cup of life without worry, believing that God knows all about you and your needs and will help you to overcome the challenges that may come your way. There is nothing too large for God to handle. If you place all your concerns into God's hands, He will remove them for you. While you are worrying, trying to figure problems out, God has already taken care of it for you. Just have faith in God, and ask Him to cover you with His precious blood from the crown of your head to the soles of your feet, then walk by faith, not by sight. The answers to your prayers will be revealed to you through blessings and miracles.

It was because of her faith in Jesus that the woman with the issue of blood touched the hem of His garment and was healed. Can you imagine her faith the size of a mustard seed was so strong that the disciples could not stop her from touching Jesus? Her faith was infallible, and because of that faith, her mountain, which was the issue of blood, was removed. Your infallible faith in Jesus will allow God to work miracles in your life; doors will be opened that no man can close. Carry the shield of faith at all times in all that you do, and watch the doors open for you.

The *helmet of salvation* is the symbolic crown of thorns placed on Christ's head, a part of his cup to bear for you and I. Salvation is your covering for the remission of your sins. John 3:16 says, "For God so loved the world that he gave His only begotten Son that who so ever believeth in Him shall not parish but have ever lasting life." Your soul is redeemed of your sins because Jesus suffered and died so that we may have everlasting life. God sacrificed Jesus to save our souls, our conscience, our spirit from perishing, from never-ending torment, the wrath—the lake of fire—to come after the judgment for those that did not accept Christ. Your salvation is your gift from God, for your living soul to spend eternity with God in heaven where there is no sorrow, pain, or tears. Christ paid it all for us by suffering on the cross. By accepting Jesus as your Lord and Savior, you placed the helmet of salvation on your head. Wear it, and know that you are saved.

The *sword of the Spirit* symbolizes God's Holy Word. The sword of the Spirit is unlike the sword of the tongue in which the Spirit will fight against. It is all the scriptures in the Holy Bible, the Word of God, that teaches us how to handle every situation in life, and it teaches us that there is nothing new under the sun (Ecclesiastes 1:9).

> For the Lord your God is He that goeth
> with you, to fight for you against your enemies,
> to save you. (Deuteronomy 20:4)

Then we shall walk clothed with the full armor of God by faith, internalizing every word of God by feeling and hearing the Spirit within us, guiding us not by sight but by the faith in God's promises. With faith, He will provide all of our needs, and whatsoever we ask of God, He will give unto us by His will.

> My sheep hear my voice, and I know them, and they follow me: And I give unto them eternal life; and they shall never perish, neither shall any man pluck them out of my hand. (John 10:27–28)

Listen to God when He speaks to you. The whisper that you hear when you are thinking and making decisions will guide you to the correct direction and the way that you should go. The decision is made for you; however, if you question it, you place yourself into a situation of choosing to be obedient or disobedient, which is not God's will. If you allow God's Spirit to guide you, there is no questioning, and there is no wrong decision. Dress daily in the full armor of God, and your outward adorning will be changed to reflect your heart and inner spirit.

> Whose adorning let it not be that outward adorning of plaiting the hair, and of wearing of gold, or of putting on of apparel; but let it be the hidden man of the heart, in that which is not corruptible, even the ornament of a meek and quiet spirit, which is in the sight of God of great price. (1 Peter 3:3–4)

God is not concerned with what you wear, your tangible outer attire. He is concerned with and concentrates on who you are internally. By clothing yourself in the full armor of God, spiritually exuding all of the fruit of the spirit beautifies your mind, heart, and soul for the glory of God. And by doing so has great value in the sight of God. God recognizes when you are beautiful for Christ.

Compose your internalization of Ephesians 6:13–18 and Matthew 5:13.

Wisdom

But the wisdom that is from above is first pure.
—James 3:17

For the Lord giveth wisdom: Out of his mouth
cometh knowledge and understanding.
—Proverbs 2:6

Wisdom is the principal thing; therefore get wisdom:
and with all thy getting get understanding.
—Proverbs 4:7

Exalt her, and she shall promote thee; she shall
bring thee to honour, when thou dost embrace her.
She shall give to thine head an ornament of grace:
a crown of glory shall she deliver to thee.
—Proverbs 4:8–9

Many people correlate wisdom to an elder's age, and with age come wisdom. This is correct in relation to earthly life's lessons learned; however, the Holy Bible speaks of wisdom. Obtaining her and exalting her has a different meaning. The wisdom that the Holy Bible is speaking of is pure because it comes from God without hypocrisy. It is full of mercy and peaceable with good fruit and nothing less (James 3:17). Wisdom is to know God and fear Him and to have knowledge of His doctrine and the understanding of how to apply the Scripture to your life's challenges. Upon doing so, wisdom becomes your ornament of grace and your crown of glory (Proverbs 4:8–9). The Lord God will give you from His mouth wisdom, understanding, and knowledge of how to love, respect, and fear Him (Proverbs 2:6).

Knowledge is having information regarding God's Holy Word. By becoming aware of God's Word, you will learn the difference between right and wrong; light and darkness; and love, hate, and forgiveness. Understanding is the ability to comprehend and make intelligible decisions concerning your cup of life. For example, when you should turn the other cheek or when you should speak or hold your tongue. Wisdom gives you knowledge of God's doctrine, and understanding gives you the intuition and the ability to apply it to your daily walk in life. Have you ever heard the question what would Jesus do? The Holy Spirit brings life and understanding into Jesus's teachings. The answer is Jesus would follow the will of His Father God in heaven by implementing God's doctrine and allowing His will to be done. This is the type of wisdom that we are seeking.

In my opinion, we should not fear God because we believe He will harm us. We should fear God because we know that He is all power, and without God, there is no other. We should fear God because we do not want Him to reject us and we do not want to lose His love, guidance, protection, grace, mercy, and salvation. We should be afraid of not pleasing Him and the possibility of our names not being found in the Book of Life. We should fear God because we do not want to lose eternal life with God in the kingdom of heaven.

To lose God's love is a greater punishment than spending eternity with Satan. The wrath of Satan is horrendous; however, the loss of God's love and the kingdom of heaven is a greater conviction! God is our Father, and He deserves our respect. God has commanded us to honor our father and our mother here on earth. Do you believe that He expects anything less from us in regard to honoring and respecting Him? This is the type of wisdom that is more precious than rubies that we must embrace and internalize. With wisdom, we learn that our crown of salvation is the admittance into the kingdom of heaven, and with wisdom, we should seek understanding of God's Word to know what we must do when we arrive there. God has a plan for us in heaven; with wisdom, you will understand what God's plan is.

A college degree is embraced and applauded when received; it may also be your entrance to a dream career in a Fortune 500 company; however, it is not your entrance into the kingdom of heaven. The effort that was put forth into studying to get your bachelor's, master's, or doctorate degree is the same effort that you should put forth to gain wisdom and understanding for the entrance into the kingdom of heaven.

Proverbs 8:11 says, "For wisdom is better than rubies; and all the things that may be desired are not to be compared to it." All material things that are desired, if received, can be taken away or used until there is no further need. Wisdom does not have an expiration date and cannot be taken away; it can be built upon for the edifying of Christ, and there is no comparison to edifying God.

Think of receiving a degree of wisdom and understanding of God's Holy Word that is taught and conferred to you by God. The only textbook needed is the Holy Bible. The degree will propel you into a realm of eternal life much higher than the achievement of receiving any other degree. The degree in wisdom that you can earn is from God. God is the President, Chancellor and Provost with the highest degree unattainable by man (the Creator). He knows all and teaches all. Many of you may have burned the midnight oil to earn your degree; that is the same type of due diligence you should put forth into studying God's Word. When you open your eyes in the morning and before you retire at night, have the burning desire in your heart to gain wisdom. God will not tempt us; however, we may be tested just like Job. Satan is here on earth roaming, looking to see whom he can devour. God gives us the ability to choose between right and wrong. If you make the wrong decision and fail, that was your will, not God's, because God does not fail. We have to study His Word continuously, knowing that in the cup of life, there will always be temptation because Satan is all around us. Know this and understand how to recognize him and what to do to make him flee.

If we are not abiding in God's Word, we are not growing in wisdom. The wisdom that we receive from God is pure. If you believe and ask God as Solomon did, God will give you wisdom. You must have faith in receiving your request. James 1:5 says, "If any of you lack wisdom, let him ask of God, that giveth to all men liberally, and upbraideth not; and it shall be given him." I ask, what does it take for a Christian to become holy? I have never asked that question to anyone before; however, I have learned that "knowledge of the Holy is understanding" (Proverbs 9:10). After reading that scripture, I have come to the conclusion that we must become holy to gain understanding. First Peter 1:16 says, "Because it is written, be ye holy; for I am holy." You may be wondering what is the process to become holy. God said, "Ye shall therefore sanctify yourselves, and ye shall be holy" (Leviticus 11:44). You will find information regarding your walk toward holiness in 2 Timothy 2. By reading the second chapter in its entirety and paying close attention to all the verses, you will read that God will give you understanding. You will also find out how to become sanctified and ultimately how to become holy in your Christian journey!

The Ten Commandments

---

1. "Thou shalt have no other Gods before Me" (Exodus 20:3).
2. "Thou shalt not make unto thee any graven image, or any likeness of any thing that is in heaven above or that is in the earth beneath, or that is in the water under the earth" (Exodus 20:4).
3. "Thou shalt not take the name of the Lord thy God in vain; for the Lord will not hold him guiltless that taketh his name in vain" (Exodus 20:7).
4. "Remember the Sabbath day, to keep it Holy" (Exodus 20:8).
5. "Honour thy father and thy mother: that thy days may be long upon the land which the Lord thy God giveth thee" (Exodus 20:12).
6. "Thou shalt not kill" (Exodus 20:13).
7. "Thou shalt not commit adultery" (Exodus 20:14).
8. "Thou shalt not steal" (Exodus 20:15).
9. "Thou shalt not bear false witness against thy neighbour" (Exodus 20:16).
10. "Thou shalt not covet thy neighbour's house, thou shalt not covet thy neighbour's wife, nor his manservant, nor his maidservant, nor his ox, nor his ass, nor anything that is thy neighbour's" (Exodus 20:17).

Blessed are they that do His commandments, that they may have right to the tree of life, and may enter in through the gates into the city.
—Revelation 22:14

Jesus's Commandments

Jesus said unto him, thou shalt love the Lord thy God with
all thy heart, and with all thy soul, and with all thy mind.
—Matthew 22:37

And the second is like unto it, Thou shalt
love thy neighbour as thyself.
—Matthew 22:39

A new commandment I give unto you, that ye love one
another; as I have loved you, that ye also love one another.
—John 13:34

My Children, let us not love in word, neither
in tongue, but in deed and in truth.
—1 John 3:18

Love One Another

As I think about the meaning of love, I take a deep breath, not because the subject of love is challenging. I breathe in deeply because to love in the manner that Christ has commanded, you must be committed to love God with the passion of truth, faith, and spirit and to love with all your heart, mind, and soul (Matthew 22:37). My exhale was the realization and understanding that Christ wants you and I to love God with every gift that we are made of.

The new commandment that Christ has given us, in part says, "That ye love one another as I have loved you." By loving one another as Christ has asked us to, He will recognize you and me as his disciples (John 13:34–35). I am one of Christ's disciples, and I am praying that if you do not recognize yourself as one of God's disciples, you become one. Jesus wants us to love one another in deed and in truth (1 John 3:18). Jesus has been our example of love and has proven His love to God and to us, all in deed and truth. Christ paid for our salvation with both deed and truth to God.

My calling is to explain the essence of love that we must give to follow Christ's commandments. Our love can never be of the same intensity as Jesus's love because we simply do not possess the ability to love like Christ although we must continuously try to love like Jesus with every fiber of our being. The human love that we are capable of giving is conditional; no matter how hard we may try, we are not perfect. God is perfect, and He loves unconditionally without wavering. We must continue to strive to give that same kind of love because it is God's will, and He wants us to be perfect (Matthew 5:48). We are commanded to love our neighbor as ourselves. Let's think about that for a moment. Now ask yourself, "Do I love myself?" If your answer is no, then you must ask God to teach you how to spiritually love yourself. If you do not love yourself, how can you love someone else? If you do love yourself, then you are capable of loving others. Have you ever prepared dinner for someone and given your guest the most succulent and tender steak because you wanted him or her to enjoy it? That is one of many examples of "love thy neighbor as thyself." A more passionate example of love is when you hear in the news that a person became a kidney donor to a stranger, giving him or her one of their kidneys and gifting him or her prolonged life. That is a beautiful example of love one another in deed.

Our love today may be warm and giving albeit it may wax cold tomorrow, depending on the challenges that our personal cup of life has handed to us. Are you able to love the person that may have hurt you or someone else you love deeply, or will you tell yourself to never forgive them? If you have forgiven them, can you truly say that you will continue to love them? Can you turn the other cheek, or if something has been stolen from you, will you also give them another object to take with them? It was easy for me to ask those questions, and to be honest, in reality, the questions may be hard for anyone to answer truthfully unless they have been in one of those situations.

Because Jesus is love, He forgave those that persecuted Him. Christ continued to love the soldier that pierced Him in the side, causing water and blood to flow from his body. He continued to love them when they placed a crown of thorns on His head and nailed Him to the cross. Because Jesus passionately loves and honors His Father, God in Heaven, and loves us as He loves Himself, He stayed on the cross and did not come down. Christ did not curse, smite, or bring any harm to anyone that participated in His crucifixion. Jesus asked His Father in heaven to forgive them. Luke 23:34 says, "Then said Jesus, Father, forgive them; for they know not what they do. And they parted his raiment and cast lots."

Jesus is our example of love in truth and in deed. For that reason, we are asked to truthfully love in all our deeds, such as prayer, praise, bless, serve, give, teach, work, and chastise. The type of love that Christ gives conquers all. Internalize the power of love that Jesus has given us, and pray to God, asking that He give you the strength, fortitude, and understanding to love in the same manner.

Jesus sacrificed His life for us. Can we sacrifice a small portion of our existence to show love and deed for our family, friends, and for those in need that we do not know? Can you forgive your brother, sister, or a stranger no matter how terribly they may have hurt you? Can you forgive someone that may have taken the life of your loved one? If you want to love like Christ, you must forgive like Christ. According to Scripture, Peter asked Jesus how often should he forgive his brother that has sinned against him, and Christ's response to Peter is found in Matthew 18:22: "I say not unto thee, until seven times: but, until seventy times seven." Love is also forgiving, and Jesus said, "If you love me, keep my commandments" (John 14:15).

You must continue to strive passionately with every fiber of your being to love one another as Jesus has commanded us to do. If you should wax cold in this area, warm your heart by feeling the love from Christ, taking His yoke upon you, and allowing the spirit of love to guide your heart, mind, and soul. For as long as there is breath in your body, you will be challenged with loving one another as Jesus has commanded.

God's Will

Saying, Father, if thou be willing, remove this cup from
me: nevertheless not my will, but thine, be done.
—Luke 22:42

Teach me to do thy will; for thou art my God: thy spirit
is good; lead me into the land of uprightness.
—Psalm 143:10

For whosoever shall do the will of God, the same
is my brother, and my sister, and mother.
—Mark 3:35

Jesus's respect for God is shown in Luke 22:42. He acknowledges God's will by saying, "Thine will be done." Jesus was on earth to do God's will. He is our example of how we should recognize and respect God while understanding that we are not in control. To totally submit yourself to God's will, you will need to acquire the desire to trust, obey, and listen to God. Resist the devil's temptations that causes sin and Satan's spirit of doubt that will lead you into the wrong direction and against God's will. Then ask God to reveal to you what His will is for you in your life.

While you are trying to determine what you should do, God has already planned it out for you. Have you ever been interviewed for a position and were not selected? The rejection may have hurt a bit, causing you to lose your self-confidence; however, I want to remind you that doubt and low self-esteem are emotions from Satan to bring you down. With patience and faith in God, you will receive a better position. Your ram is in the bush and waiting for you to claim it. Think of it this way: the first job was not God's will for you; it was what you wanted. When God is involved, your reward is greater than your request.

By asking God if it is His will, you are acknowledging that you want to do and become what God has planned for your life. Remaining prayerful in all that you do will allow you to wait for the Holy Spirit to give you the directions to God's will. God will never tempt you to do wrong or mislead you. Most importantly, you must ask God to teach you how to do His will and ask God to lead you to the land of the uprighteousness (Psalm 143:10).

Therefore, you must not be conformed to the world. To do God's will, you must utilize prayer and patience then wait on God to answer. To accept God's will, you must renew your mind, internalize, and understand that you are not in control. God is the Head of all creation and decisions to be made. Allow God's will to dominate in all that you do, and it will be perfect and acceptable in His sight. No person is perfect; however, God has instructed us to be perfect (Matthew 5:48). Whosoever does the will of God, Jesus has promised that they will be the same as His brother, sister, and mother (Matthew 12:50).

PART 4

PRAYER

Prayer

Men ought always to pray, and not to faint.
—Luke 18:1

Again I say unto you that if two of you shall agree on earth as touching any thing that they shall ask, it shall be done for them of my Father which is in heaven. For where two or three are gathered together in my name, there am I in the midst of them.
—Matthew 18:19–20

If my people who are called by my name will humble themselves and pray and seek my face and turn from their wicked ways, then will I hear from heaven and forgive them their sin and heal their land.
—2 Chronicles 7:14

Personal prayer is between you and God. Allow yourself to become dependent upon your communication with God. Look forward to praying and talking with Him daily. Scripture says, "Train up a child in the way he should go and when he is old, he will not depart from it" (Proverbs 22:6). Are we to become converted as little children and train ourselves to pray? Matthew 18:3 says, "And said, verily I say unto you, except ye be converted, and become as little children, ye shall not enter into the Kingdom of heaven." I am suggesting that you train yourself to pray and ensure that your prayers are fervent and frequent, forming an unbreakable relationship with God. Locate a private area where you can bow down or prostrate, and humble yourself before God with no spectators.

Before you begin your prayer, ask God for forgiveness, then take a moment to meditate and acknowledge God by giving Him honor and praises, bringing forward to your conscience the respect and love that you have for God. Make it known to God while preparing yourself for the Holy Spirit to assist you. Petition the Holy Spirit to help with your infirmities by giving you assistance with your prayer (Romans 8:26). Become closer to God, feel His presence, concentrate on Him, then open your heart and mind, then let your praises and love for God flow from your lips in secret.

Matthew 6:6 says in part, "Pray to thy Father in secret, and thy Father which seeth in secret shall reward thee openly." Thank God for your existence and for creating the person that you are. Share with God that you are thankful to Him for sacrificing His Son, Jesus Christ, for the redemption of your sins, and acknowledge that you know that God is the Provider of all your needs. It is very important to know how to communicate with God in prayer.

Jesus has said in John 14:6, "I am the way, the truth and the life no man cometh unto the Father, but by me." After reading the scripture and internalizing it, I understand it to mean that Christ the Son of God is Truth and Life. After accepting Christ as your Savior, you will be accepted by His Father. By doing so, you will have a line of communication to God through Jesus. For those reasons, I have determined that an illustrious salutation should always be used when approaching Jesus and God in prayer, and when closing your prayer, it is correct to say, "In Jesus's name, I pray," acknowledging that you know that you must go through Christ to be with the Father. You should also end your prayer by saying "Amen," which confirms it is so.

By proceeding and ending in this manner, you are acknowledging God the Father and Jesus because He is the Way. I just mentioned that I determined it to be correct to pray in Jesus's name; however, I want you to find it to be correct, and the proof can be found in John 14:13–14. Think about it. Are you able to enter into the White House and walk directly into the presidential oval office and start a conversation with the president of the United States? The answer to that question is no. You will have to comply with official protocol. That may include a background check for security clearance in addition to other security requirements, then you must have an appointment, and if approved, someone will escort you to the president of the United States. God has perfected the line of communication. We can reach God in prayer by going through His Son, Jesus.

After prayer, listen and pay attention. God will answer your prayers according to His purpose and will. God does not want us to pray repetitiously. He knows what your needs are before you ask. You can ask God for anything in prayer. When you pray, ask God if it is His will. Let it be done. Please be careful when praying. God wants to hear from you in happiness with praises to Him as well as in times of need.

For example, both parties in the relationship, as in a marriage, must equally commit to the relationship that is worthy of having. We should not expect God to be committed to us if we are not totally committed to Him. Prayers are powerful. Ensure that you are careful in what you pray for, and remember, others can be blessed when you pray for them. Pray for your husband, your family, your friends, your pastor and his family, and pray for the sick and the leaders of the world and the people of the world.

By asking God to step in and soften the heart of your enemy, God can change that foe into a friend. Free your mind of other thoughts, and humble yourself, and boldly approach God's throne of grace and mercy. I am by no means suggesting that you do not pray for yourself. I am asking that you pray fervently for others also.

Speak to God; bring Him into your heart. Feel the love you have for Him, and know that He has so much more love for you. You should pray privately away from all distractions. God deserves respect from you in all that you do, including prayer. There is no other on earth that is more important than God. Jesus has given us instructions on how to pray, which is found in the book of Matthew 6:5–8, followed by the perfect prayer from Jesus, giving His disciples the words that we should pray, which are found in the book of Matthew 6:9–13.

You cannot bargain with God by asking Him to give you something and you will do something in return for Him. Quid pro quo is not the way to pray; that is an insult to God. If it is God's will, He will provide your needs; however, He may not provide all your wants if your want is something that you can achieve yourself.

The following is how Jesus instructed us to pray because we too are disciples:

"Our Father which art in heaven, hallowed be thy name. Thy kingdom come. Thy will be done in earth, as it is in Heaven. Give us this day our daily bread. And forgive us our debts, as we forgive our debtors. And lead us not into temptation, but deliver us from evil. For thine is the kingdom, and the power and the glory, forever. Amen."

According to Scripture, men should always pray and not faint (Luke 18:1). This scripture is short in terms of words but powerful when you call on the name of Jesus. I say power because my brother Edward said a prayer at the time of his passing. It was not the Lord's Prayer. I don't believe there was enough time. The only words he could utter during his massive heart attack were "Jesus, take me away." I brought this up to say Edward did not faint. He prayed, and I believe his prayer was heard by God. No matter what you are going through, you should always call on the name of Jesus.

If the prayer of one man can be heard, can you imagine the power of the payer if more than one person is praying in the same accord? You will not have to imagine. Scripture says, "For where two or three gather together in my name there, am I in the midst of them" (Matthew 18:20). The world would be a better place if we all could change our sinful ways, humble ourselves, and pray on one accord, touching and agreeing while seeking God's face. God will hear us and heal our land. When I say our land, I am including all land that God has created on this earth. I am speaking of praying for the entire world where Satan has dominion. Scripture says that if we can do that, God will heal the land (2 Chronicles 7:14). Satan is busy preventing us from achieving this goal, but I ask you to pray and not faint.

In my opinion, there is no prayer more powerful than the prayer that Jesus has given us. It covers all our needs and acknowledges God and His glory. It is the prayer that I learned as a child; however, as an adult, I have learned how to pray different types of prayers coming from my heart. I thank and praise Jesus. Hallelujah for giving us the Lord's Prayer. He has shown us how to begin, the substance to include, and how to end our prayer. If you have never given thought about the true meaning of this prayer, I ask that you take a moment and internalize with writing what the Lord's Prayer means to you. I thought about this some time ago and decided to internalize the Lord's Prayer, and this is what it means to me.

My Internalization of the Lord's Prayer

"Our Father which art in heaven." Jesus is saying that God is the Father of everyone. Jesus was addressing God in the beginning of the prayer with the word *our*, acknowledging that God is more than His Father. God is our Father also. Jesus also recognized God as a supernatural being by telling us that God is in heaven, acknowledging that heaven is a place we should believe in. Jesus fed us this information in the first six words of the prayer.

"Hallowed be thy name." Jesus is informing us that God's name is holy, exalted in perfection and righteousness. His name should not be spoken in vain, and God is worthy of our continuous and complete devotion with profound reverence.

"Thy kingdom come." Jesus is acknowledging heaven as God's kingdom with the use of the word *Thy*, meaning "God's." I am praying to be allowed to enter into the kingdom of heaven and to live in the holy city where the walls are of jasper and the foundation is garnished with precious stones and the twelve gates are twelve pearls and the streets are pure gold with a pure river flowing from the throne. On either side of the river is the tree of life for healing of the nations. However, to enter in, we must all be transformed by God from flesh to spirit.

"Thy will be done in earth as it is in heaven." Jesus is speaking to God, acknowledging that whatever God's will is, it will be done in earth and also in heaven. We should be asking ourselves these two questions: the first being has God told us what His will is for us on earth? The second question is did God tell us what His will is for us in heaven? By telling us to pray, "Thy will be done," Jesus is saying to God, "Whatever it is that You want Me to do, I will do." God has given us instructions on how He wants us to live here in earth and in heaven. The Ten Commandments from God are our instructions for living in earth. In all our prayers to God, we must recognize, if it is His will, it will be done. God has given us the ability to explore great possibilities of professions and careers during our lifetime, and if it's God's will, it will happen. When I pray this prayer, I am saying that I will do God's will, whatever it may be in earth and in heaven. It is also written that in heaven, God's will is for us to praise Him (Psalm 150:1).

"Give us this day our daily bread." The bread that we are praying for is not food for our stomachs. In Luke 4:4, Jesus said, "Man shall not live by bread alone, but by every word of God." God knows all our needs; God has given us His Son, Jesus, as our bread to consume (John 6:51).

"Forgive us our debts as we forgive our debtors." Matthew 6:14–15 says, "For if ye forgive men their trespasses, your heavenly Father will also forgive you. But if ye forgive not men trespasses, neither will your Father forgive your trespasses." This scripture is clear as glass and easy to understand. No matter what pain someone has caused me, I will forgive him or her because I too am a sinner and will continually ask God to forgive me for my sins. Forgiveness is a virtue that we must obtain and internalize it within our hearts to become more like Christ. Can you imagine asking God for forgiveness and He said no? Forgiveness is also the light of love shining in your heart. It is easy to forgive someone that you love because you already have a bond. We must be able to forgive with love even when there is no bond. Christ said that we must forgive "seventy times seven" (Matthew 18:21).

Romans 3:23 says, "For all have sinned, and come short of the glory of God." I am constantly praying and asking for God's forgiveness because we are born into sin.

If you do not forgive, then God will not forgive you!

"Lead us not into temptation." We are asking God to guide us away from evil, to order our steps by allowing us to follow Him because God cannot be tempted. According to Scripture, temptation is common to man, and God would not allow temptation to be more than we can handle. God has given us the ability to escape (1 Corinthians 10:13).

"Deliver us from evil." We are asking God for protection to keep us safe from the fiery dart of Satan and from all his evil principalities.

"For Thine is the kingdom." God is the Kingdom; everything that is within it—righteousness, peace, and joy in the Holy Ghost—all belongs to God (Romans 14:17).

"And the power." No man is greater or have the power of God, as stated in the book of Colossians 1:13–17:

> Who hath delivered us from the power of darkness, and hath translated us into the kingdom of his dear Son: In Whom we have redemption through his blood, even the forgiveness of sins: Who is the image of the invisible God, the firstborn of every creature: For by him were all things created, that are in heaven, and that are in earth, visible and invisible, whether they be thrones, or dominions, or principalities, or powers: all things were created by him and for him: And he is before all things, and by him all things consist.

"And the glory." God, You are the glory of all magnificent things in existence because of Your power of creation.

Psalm 104:31 says, "The glory of the Lord shall endure for ever: the Lord shall rejoice in his works."

"Forever." This means eternity, without end, infinitely.

"Amen." So be it. It is so; a solemn confirmation and belief.

The Lord's Prayer that Jesus gave us is the masterpiece of all prayers. It recognizes, acknowledges, honors, and exalts God. It humbles and asks for the Word of God, forgiveness, protection, and direction. It glorifies and confirms our belief.

Take time to read Matthew 6:9–13, and pray it aloud, understanding and internalizing every word spoken, then write down your internalization of the prayer.

Compose your internalization of Matthew 6:9–13.

Different Types of Prayers

When you pray, bow down and humbly submit yourself to God, and boldly approach His throne of grace so that you may obtain mercy (Hebrews 4:16). Ask the Holy Spirit to assist you with your prayer. Prayer is your communication with God. Open up your heart, and pour out your innermost thoughts, needs, and concerns; then end your prayer, acknowledging that you are praying in Jesus's name.

There are many different types of prayers. I would like to introduce to you five types of prayers, beginning with the most used prayer, which in my opinion is the prayer of petition. The petition prayer is the most frequently prayed prayer; it is the prayer of asking God to fulfill your needs or wants. Many people pray this type of prayer. It is good to know God's Word and the promises He has made to you. With studying, you will learn what those promises are, and you can include them in your prayer request. God promised us that He would never leave us nor forsake us. This promise can be found in Hebrews 13:5. You can use this scripture when asking God for strength and His presence in your life.

Second Peter 1:4 says, "Whereby are given unto us exceeding great and precious promises: that by these ye might be partakers of the divine nature, having escaped the corruption that is in the world through lust." Study God's Word, and remember the many promises that He has made, believing as you pray, asking God to bless you with His promise of your need if it is His will.

When I pray this type of prayer, I would say, "Father God, I come to You as humble as I know how, thanking and praising Your holy name. Hallelujah. Lord, in Your Holy Word, You said, 'Ask and it shall be given,' and that You would never leave us nor forsake us. Lord, I am asking that You send the Comforter to help me with my grief and to ease my pain. Lord, I need You now, and I am asking that You bless me in a mighty way if it is Your will."

The shortest petition prayer in the Bible is "Lord, save me" (Matthew 14:30).

We have been instructed in 2 Chronicles 7:14 on how we should pray. We cannot demand anything from God, and we must humble ourselves and seek God, not asking for worldly gain from Him. When we ask of Him, our request should be "Father God in heaven, please give me the spirit and strength to be like You, O Lord. Please help me to become holy." Let God know that you want to walk in holiness in His path of righteousness. If we are in tune with the adversary, why should God answer our prayers? We cannot serve two masters.

As you mature in Christ, you will begin to offer up prayers from your innermost spirit, thinking only of God. This type of prayer is called *adoration*. It is a prayer of praising God, blessing His name, lifting Him up, glorifying God, and letting Him know that you love Him and adore Him. You are not asking for anything. You are letting God know that you appreciate Him.

First Samuel 2:2 says, "There is none holy as the Lord: for there is none beside thee; neither is there any rock like our God."

Praying for others is called *intercession* prayers; they are prayers to God offered on behalf of someone else. For example, this type of prayer is given when someone asks you to pray for them or if someone approaches the pastor to ask him and members of the church to pray for them. You may also pray for someone without them asking or knowing. Prayers are offered on their behalf, asking God to come into their life and heal or handle all their needs, whatever they may be. The Holy Spirit intercedes for all of us when we pray.

> Who is he that condemeth? It is Christ that died, yea rather, that is risen again, who is even at the right hand of God, who also make intercessions for us. (Romans 8:34)

Jesus prayed an intercession prayer while hanging on the cross.

> Then said Jesus, Father, forgive them; for they know not what they do. And they parted his raiment, and cast lots. (Luke 23:34)

Thanking God for His goodness, mercy, healing, and blessings is a prayer of *thanksgiving*, found in Ephesians 5:20: "Giving thanks always for all things unto God and the Father in the name of our lord Jesus Christ."

> In everything give thanks: for this is the will of God in Christ Jesus concerning you. (1 Thessalonians 5:18)

You can pray and let God know that you are thankful by naming everything and every blessing that you have received from Him. This is a good time to thank Him for the prayers that He has answered for you. In my prayers of thanksgiving, I thank God for His Son, Jesus Christ, who died on the cross for my sin. I thank Him for watching over me as I sleep and slumber and waking me in the morning, clothing me in my right mind. I thank Him for my family and for keeping my family from hurt, harm, and danger. I thank Him for my health and strength. I thank Him for the air that I breathe. You see, every part of your being is from God, including every hair on your head, and you should be thankful. Start with prayer of adoration for God, acknowledging His power and might.

I thank God for giving me wisdom and understanding that He is God. I also thank Him for all the blessings that I have received and for the forgiveness of my sins.

When you truly know God, you will learn to thank and praise Him for the air that you breathe, for the sun that warms the earth, for the moon and the stars that give light to midnight's darkness, and for the rain that fills every body of water that cool our lips when we are thirsty. God has made earth habitable and beautiful. I can never thank Him enough for the infinite blessings that He has and will bestow upon me. God is so good that praising Him will forever be on my lips.

The *mediation* prayer is what Jesus asked us to do. This is the type of prayer that does not come easy when someone provokes you. You will have to listen to God's Spirit speaking to you. You will have to resist the evil spirit that will tell you to strike back with an evil tongue; instead, pray for the offenders and ask God to bless them in a mighty way.

> But I say unto you, Love your enemies, bless them that curse you, do good to them that hate you, and pray for them which despitefully use you, and persecute you; That ye may be the children of your Father which is in heaven; for he maketh his sun to rise on the evil and on the good, and sendeth rain on the just and on the unjust. (Matthew 5:44–45)

When you pray for your enemies and ask God to bless them, you are becoming the mediator between your own adversaries to bring about peace because it is God's will. You may be surprised in the blessing you will receive.

Blessings

Saying, Amen: Blessing, and glory, and wisdom, and thanksgiving, and honour, and power, and might, be unto our God for ever and ever. Amen.
—Revelation 7:12

But my God shall supply all your need according to his riches in glory by Christ Jesus.
—Philippians 4:19

And were continually in the temple, praising and blessing God, Amen.
—Luke 24:53

A great number of people can be selfish when it comes to blessings. I say that because we as people want to be blessed all of the time, and I ask, who wouldn't? Have you ever truly thought about your blessings? We should learn to think of blessings in a different light. As a young child, I learned from my brother Victor what it means to be blessed. I remember, he and I were standing for an extremely long time waiting for a train to arrive. I was tired, then I noticed a person sitting in a wheelchair and said aloud, "I wish I had a wheelchair to sit on." My brother immediately corrected me sternly and explained to me that I was blessed to be able to stand and not need assistance. I thought about what he had said the entire train ride, and his statement remains with me to this day. I have learned over the years from that day to recognize blessings in my life. Have you considered asking yourself, "What can I do to help others?" Or thought of how you can bless someone instead of praying for God to bless them? What is overlooked most times is the fact that we all are being blessed every day by an unselfish God, and we can bless others in many ways also.

When we awake in the morning and open our eyes, we are blessed. When our family is safe and there is no bad news, we are blessed. If we have our health and strength and are cognitively sound, then yes, we have been blessed. These are a few of the blessings that may be overlooked by anyone. We see the accomplishments of others and say that they are lucky, which is incorrect. The correct thought should be, "They are blessed." If you can find it in your heart to bless someone, it does not have to be a monetary blessing; it can be a baked blessing, an errand blessing, a babysitting blessing, a tutoring blessing, and the list is infinite with ways that you can bless others. When you see that someone needs a blessing, if you can help them with their situation, bless them and pray for them as well.

Scripture says, "I will bless the Lord," meaning, you and I should also bless the Lord by invoking divine care (Psalm 34:34). I want to address the blessings that we should give God; He deserves to be blessed continually by all His children. We can thank Him by blessing His name; by saying, "Lord, I bless Your holy name; by saying, "Glory, hallelujah to You, God," which is an elevated praise to God; and also by recognizing and saying, "All power, glory, and honor are Yours, almighty Father. I thank You, and I bless You Lord, in the name of Jesus."

The message that I would like for you to receive from this section is that blessings go both ways. When praises and blessings go up to God in heaven, blessings will come down from God to you. Scripture says in Philippians 4:19, "God shall supply all our needs according to His riches in glory by Jesus Christ." I ask that you read again the section about the glory of God. Can you imagine the blessings that can be waiting for you? Now think of the mighty blessing you will and have already received. No one other than God can bless you like God's riches in glory by Jesus Christ. Most importantly, I ask that while you are receiving blessings from God, you also bless God!

It is unfortunate that some people may not know when they are or have been blessed and how to protect and appreciate their blessings. Some people may only recognize their answers to prayers as blessings; however, blessings can be found in some of the most unfortunate situations. Remember, life experiences can always be worse, and it is a blessing when the cup of life is sweet.

I remember many years ago, my family owned a midsize honey-gold sedan. After our family outing one evening, we arrived home and parked the Lancer in a parking lot, facing the side of a brick building. The next morning, we found the car beneath a pile of rubble, crushed by the entire brick wall. The entire sidewall of the building had fallen onto the car and smashed the top half, leaving the entire roof of the car, windshield, and all windows covered with bricks lying on the seats. The only visual parts of the car that could be seen were the lower half of the doors, fender, and tires. The car had been demolished; it looked like a golden dutch baby with wheels. The car was totaled. My heart dropped when I saw what had happened. My first thought was "This is really terrible." I actually mentally visualized a dark storm cloud, and it seemed to be consuming my mind because the Lancer was our only car. I'm sure the adversary, Satan, was happy; he wanted me to become depressed. Then the Holy Spirit told me to find the silver lining in that cloud. It was then that I remembered my entire family of six was in the car when we parked it the night before, and that the bricks could have fallen onto the car with the entire family inside, injuring us all, or maybe the accident could have been fatal.

It was then that I realized that we were blessed, and God had placed his hedge of protection around us, allowing us to exit the car safely before the disaster. That dark cloud was Satan trying to cloud my understanding and realization that God protected us. The Holy Spirit showed me how to look past the darkness and see the beautiful bright silver lining in it; we were protected by God's grace and mercy. I just needed to realize it and count my blessings, all six of them, because we were not harmed. That was one of the most beautiful blessings I have ever received, and I continue to thank God.

That is only one example of my blessings. I have received many blessings from God, and I recognize them all and thank Him for the blessings that He has bestowed upon my family and me. God is a great and giving God and blesses us all the time. I want you to know that even though something less than desirable may have happened in your life, search your heart and mind to find the real blessing in the dark situation, find the silver lining, and thank God for your blessing.

LADWYINA TOLAR-SLATER

Expound upon the many blessings that God has bestowed upon your life and how you can bless God and others.

Praise in the Beauty of Holiness

> I will freely sacrifice unto thee: I will praise
> thy name, O Lord; for it is good.
> —Psalm 54:6

> Let them praise the name of the Lord: for His name alone
> is excellent; his glory is above the earth and heaven.
> —Psalm 148:13

> And whatsoever ye do in word or deed
> (do) all in the name of the Lord Jesus,
> giving thanks to God and the Father by him.
> —Colossians 3:17

In layman's terms, to *praise* can be defined as the approval of someone. I ask, who are we to approve God? I do not believe that we can pass judgment to approve or disapprove God; however, I do firmly believe that we should praise God to show our gratitude, acceptance, and love for Him. Praise defined, as a religious term, is to exalt through words and song, giving magnification or glorification and acknowledging the perfections of all the works of God. I have given great thought regarding the subject of praise and have come to the conclusion for my understanding that praises coming from my heart and mind by speaking to God is showing great love and appreciation for His sacrifices. We in turn should also make sacrifices to God.

In the book of Romans 12:1–2, we are told to present our bodies as a living sacrifice, and Psalm 54:6 tells us to "freely sacrifice."

Our sacrifice should come freely. I asked myself what type of sacrifice is God looking for from us. I located an answer to my question in Hebrews 13:15 that says, "By him therefore let us offer the sacrifice of praise to God continually, that is, the fruit of our lips giving thanks to his name." Once again, God has blessed us with an easy sacrifice if we love Him. Isn't it proper to say, "Thank You, Lord, for all that You have done" in the most magnified and glorious way possible?

God wants us to praise His holy name continually in spirit and truth by reminding ourselves that all glory and honor are God's and the complete essence and existence of our being is because of Him. Say it to God; let Him know that you do understand that He is almighty. Why should we need to be guided and told to give God praises, a handclap, or to stand on our feet as recognition to God? The answer is we should not have to be told to praise God; it should be done freely with the desire so great in our hearts that it will move us to jump up from our seats, raising our hands as though we are touching the hem of His garment in the sky while lifting our voices to say, "Hallelujah, thank You, God."

Why are you praising God? You are praising God because He is worthy to be praised, according to the Scripture. Revelation 4:11 says, "Thou are worthy, O Lord, to receive glory and honour and power: For thou has created all things, and for thy pleasure they are and were created."

We should also praise and appreciate God because He is loving, holy, and forgiving. He has set an example for us to follow. Christ as our Mentor is greater than any other mentor. We should praise Jesus because He has blessed us with His love by gifting us with salvation by dying on the cross for our sins. Psalm 150:2 says, "Praise him for his mighty acts; praise him according to his excellent greatness." Let the praises for God forever be on your lips.

Internalize Psalm 150:2 and expound on your praises to God.

Worship in the Beauty of Holiness

Give unto the Lord the glory due unto his name;
worship the Lord in the beauty of holiness.
—Psalm 29:2

But the hour cometh, and now is, when the true worshippers shall worship the Father in spirit and in truth: for the Father seeketh such to worship him. God is a Spirit: and they that worship him must worship him in spirit and in truth.
—John 4:23–24

O come, let us worship and bow down: let
us kneel before the Lord our maker.
—Psalm 95:6

I sat with my hands folded and studied the word *worship* located at the top of the page. I am pondering of a way to present to you my innermost thoughts and my understanding of worship; however, the Holy Spirit has guided me to include the scripture which states in part, "Worship the Lord in the beauty of holiness" (Psalm 29:2). I realize that the word worship, in detail, is more complex than the definition; it includes a process of approaching the actual service, which has distinct qualities that God seeks from us. I asked myself, where in the Bible is God seeking anything, and what is God seeking from us? God is Alpha and Omega and the reason that all exists; He has given us the world. With that thought in mind, I began to believe that God did not seek anything from us. Then I began my research and located a scripture that once again speaks of truth, which reminds me of the belt of truth in the full armor of God. God wants truth, which is the opposite teaching of the adversary. This scripture tells us what God seeks from us: "God is seeking true worshippers to worship Him in spirit and truth" (John 4:23–24). God is seeking the spirit of truth in our worship service from true believers, not pretenders, going through the motions. God knows His true worshippers and hears their praises.

Jesus is the Truth and the Life. We have been informed by Scripture to put on the full armor of God. As a reminder, we must approach God, girted in truth, when we bow down to worship Him. God knows your heart; you must approach your worship service with love and truth with your thoughts remaining on God and no one else. We must give God our entire heart, mind, and soul as we worship Him freely. While worshipping God, you must block out your surroundings, your workday, your family, your finances, and all other distractions. It is time for a personal relationship with God. By worshipping Him in truth, you are letting God know that He is above all others and above all concerns. God expects to hear from you, and He will listen as you glorify, honor, magnify, and bless His holy name.

You must also approach your worship service in the Spirit because God is Spirit, and He is seeking His children that possess the Spirit in the beauty of holiness.

Psalm 96:9 says, "O worship the Lord in the beauty of holiness; fear before him, all the earth." This is why we must become beautiful for Christ to worship God in the way that He expects us to. God will not request you to do anything without guiding you. Didn't God instruct Moses of how to build the Ark of the Covenant to house the Ten Commandments? The answer to that question is yes, and God has also given us instructions on how to worship Him. You will please God when you approach Him in spirit and truth; God will hear you. God does not want you to worship Him with empty words from your mouth and repetition from your lips. Allow the Holy Spirit within you to guide you. Listen and become humble, beautiful, truthful, and loving, then worship the Almighty Father in heaven.

There are many ways that we worship the Lord, and we must remember to approach God in spirit, truth, and beauty of holiness with every activity that we participate in as Christians. When we participate in the holy communion, we are worshipping God by doing so in remembrance and solemn respect for Him. When we honor God with our offerings of sacrifice for righteousness, we are worshipping God; and when we honor Him with praises and songs, we are worshipping God. God wants a true worshipper; He does not want someone to just go through empty motions of dancing and singing without truthfully feeling and believing. While worshipping God, you must feel the Spirit of God within you, then worship and glorify Him with your heart, mind, and soul.

I am asking God to remove these words from my vocabulary and/or vices from me in preparation for worshipping Him in the beauty of holiness.

PART 5

FRUIT OF THE SPIRIT

Fruit of the Spirit

But the fruit of the Spirit is love, joy, peace,
longsuffering, gentleness, goodness and faith.
—Galatians 5:17

But he that is joined unto the Lord is one spirit.
—1 Corinthians 6:17

Jesus answered and said unto him, if a man love me, he will keep my words: and my Father will love him, and we will come unto him, and make our abode with him.
—John 14:23

The fruit of the Spirit are the beauty of Christ.
Internalize and become beautiful for Christ.

Love

Joy

Peace

Long-suffering

Gentleness

Goodness

Faith

Meekness

Temperance

Love

And thou shalt love the Lord thy God with all thy heart,
and with all thy soul, and with all thy mind, and with
all thy strength: This is the first commandment.
—Mark 12:30

And the second is like, namely this,
Thou shalt love thy neighbour as thyself. There is none
other commandment greater than these.
—Mark 12:31

Thou shalt not avenge nor bear any grudge against
the children of thy people, but thou shalt love
thy neighbor as thy self: I am the Lord.
—Leviticus 19:18

Being joined with Christ in one Spirit will require dedicated work; you are headed toward understanding the spirit of love in Jesus now that you have accepted Him. You must have a strong desire to seek the Spirit of Jesus with the same passion as the disciples did. Jesus told His chosen disciples to lay down their nets and follow Him. Their nets were their security in life; it was all that they possessed, their livelihood, shelter, and food for themselves and possibly for their families. The disciples gave up everything to follow Christ.

We must lay down the world to be closer to Christ in one Spirit. This may seem hard; however, it can be achieved by embracing and internalizing the fruit of the Spirit while walking in the spirit of love. Love is what Jesus commanded, and love is what you and I need to love others as we love ourselves. It is normal for a family to love one another, but Christ is asking us to love our neighbors as we love ourselves (Mark 12:31). Can you imagine loving your neighbor that you do not know? To love them, you must get to know them. Introduce yourself, show yourself friendly, and speak with kindness in your heart and with a smile on your face. This should be practiced at church as well. Greet everyone you come in contact with a welcoming smile. Remember, God loves those whom has been cast aside, mocked, and ridiculed. Also, you should be aware that he or she is at church seeking God's love. We must love everyone we come in contact with. Who are we to judge anyone?

Always remember that you are seeking to become like Christ; to behave in any other way does not mirror Christ. When we carry an unbecoming attitude, we are acting on behalf of the adversary. To achieve the ability to love like Jesus, we must judge not and open our hearts with compassion, concern, and understanding.

In the Scripture, John 21:16 says, "He saith to him again the second time, Simon, son of Jonas, lovest thou me? He saith unto Him, yea, Lord; thou knowest that I love thee. He saith unto him, feed my sheep." The sheep that Jesus is speaking of are all of God's children, including you and me; the food that Jesus is speaking of is the gift of the Holy Word of God that will lead His sheep to everlasting life. God's love in its manifestation is our demonstration of love by the request of Jesus shown by feeding His sheep—our family, friends, and neighbors—the Word of God if they will listen.

I have noticed, on many occasions, people asking for money to buy food. In today's world, people may feel uncomfortable with giving hard-earned money to someone unknown to them. Jesus has asked us to feed His sheep. The context of feeding that Jesus is speaking of is to provide the Word of God; however, because we have learned to love like Christ, we should also provide for the needy.

My family and I were in Morocco, seated at a restaurant's outdoor patio table. Two children riding bikes came to the table asking for food. I am not sure which one of us offered up the food first; however, our table was completely emptied of the food. We had given the entire spread to the children. Of course, we were famished, and the children happened to arrive at the right time because we had not begun to eat. It was the love of God within us that fed the children. The two young boys left with the food very quickly that we did not have an opportunity to spread the Word of God verbally. But God's love was shown in its manifestation. We loved our neighbors as ourselves. Now that I think of it, the children's hunger was passed onto my family and myself until we were served again. Yes, that was love.

This is how I have loved my neighbor as I love myself as Christ commanded.

My Internalization of 1 Peter 4:13

> But rejoice, inasmuch as ye are partakers of Christ's sufferings; that, when his glory shall be revealed, ye may be glad also with exceeding joy.
> —1 Peter 4:13

But is a preposition used to introduce a statement that follows.

Rejoice is to celebrate, to show that you are happy about something.

Inasmuch as is a statement that explains limits. The limit is we did not know that we were the cause of Christ's suffering.

Ye are partakers of. We became partakers, having a share in the cause of His death, because we are sinners in the world. Christ had to bear the cross of our sins to redeem us.

Christ's sufferings. Jesus was crucified for our transgressions so that we may be healed and to fulfill the scriptures that are written in Isaiah.

Isaiah 53:5–6 says, "But he was wounded for our transgressions, He was bruised for our iniquities: the chastisement of our peace was upon him; and with his stripes we are healed."

That, when His glory shall be revealed. When I think of God's glory, I think of His resurrection and His return, His magnificence, splendor, beauty, radiance, and all of His mysteries will be made known through divine revelation.

Ye may be glad also means that we have permission to be happy also because we were the reason for Christ's crucifixion and resurrection so that the world may know that He is the Son of God.

With exceeding joy is exponentially greater than the defined meaning of joy, which is happiness; ecstatic with exceptional joy in knowing that Christ will come again and descend from heaven with the sound of the trumpet of God.

Joy

>Likewise, I say unto you, there is joy in the presence of the angels of God over one sinner that repenteth.
>—Luke 15:10

>And ye now therefore have sorrow: but I will see you again, and your heart shall rejoice, and your joy no man taketh from you.
>—John 16:22

>For the Kingdom of God is not meat and drink; but righteousness, and peace, and joy in the Holy Ghost.
>—Romans 14:17

To have joy is to have great happiness as the utmost feeling, as in ecstatic. There must have been many times in your life when you have felt joy. An engagement, the birth of a child, a graduation, a new career, a promotion, an acceptance into the university of your choice—every one of these mentioned accomplishments should give a person a feeling of joy.

Can you imagine the great joy that Christ must have had in His accomplishments when He was working for God? The many miracles of healing the sick, making the lame walk, giving sight to the blind, the feeding of multitudes, and raising the dead. Can you imagine the joy that He brought to the many people He touched? This is what Christ wants you to become: a joy provider. You may be wondering, "How can I give joy to someone?" This joy to give away is so easy in today's world. You can volunteer, you can mentor, or you can donate. Those are just a few suggestions out of many ways that you can provide joy to someone that you have come in contact with. When you think of being like Christ, you must include all the fruit of the Spirit. Jesus also wants us to bring joy to the angels of God through repentance.

I was in a brief meeting in the office of a pastor before a funeral service. The pastor and I heard laughing and playing in the sanctuary where the infant was lying in state. I looked at the pastor and asked, "Whose child is here?"

He explained to me that the child was the secretary's grandson. I became concerned because I didn't want the child to think that the deceased baby was a toy and begin playing with him. I looked at the pastor and said to him that I am going to check on the baby to make sure that he had not been disturbed. I left the office and walked quickly to the sanctuary to find that the baby in the casket was fine, and I also found the secretary's grandson dancing and playing joyfully skipping in a circle with his arms outstretched as if he were holding hands with other children. I say other children because he was not holding his hands up high. I asked him nicely, "What are you doing?" He said that he was playing with the angels. I slowly looked around, but I did not see the angels. He asked me, "Don't you see them?" I don't remember if I responded, but I had faith that if angels were involved, everything will be fine.

My worries faded, and I returned to the pastor's office, walking backward. While I continued watching him play and laugh, I was amazed, and I believed him. I knew that the angels would not let anything bad happen. After returning to the pastor's office, he asked, "Is everything okay?" I told him what I had encountered and asked him what he thought of it. His response was that he believed the child was playing with the angels. I suggested that he should go and see for himself. He said no, he did not want to disturb the angels.

I now know that the secretary's grandson had joy in the presence of the angels. I do believe that the angels were there playing with him because I saw the joy on his face and heard the laughter coming from his mouth; it was beautiful. Joy is beautiful. Recognize and embrace it.

LADWYINA TOLAR-SLATER

Lord, this is the joy You have brought to my heart.

Peace

For unto us a child is born, unto us a son is given: and
the government shall be upon his shoulder: and his
name shall be called Wonderful, Counselor, The mighty
God, The everlasting Father, The Prince of Peace.
—Isaiah 9:6

Follow peace with all men, and holiness, without
which no man shall see the Lord.
—Hebrews 12:14

Peace I leave with you, my peace I give unto you:
not as the world giveth, give I unto you. Let not
your heart be troubled, neither let it be afraid.
—John 14:27

The sound of the word *peace*, when spoken, gives me the thoughts of serenity, calm, quiet, tranquility, warmth, and rest. God is described by many of the words mentioned individually and combined, the Almighty God is the "Prince of peace" (Isaiah 9:6). Peace is the type of spirit God wants us to wake up with every morning. When Jesus told His disciples to lay down everything and follow Him, God was saying to them, "Lay down all your worries, fears, works, worldly concerns, and activities. Jesus wanted the disciples to walk in His footsteps and learn from Him. Jesus wanted to give them peace and show the disciples with actions the Gospel of peace.

Matthew 11:28 says, "Come unto me, all ye that labour and are heavy laden, and I will give you rest."

God is saying, "Follow Me, learn from Me, and walk in My steps." Give an aura, a sensation of light and peace to all that you come in contact with. God is the Prince of peace. Everyone and anything that God touches can be calmed. He can say, "Peace, be still, and the calm will come." God can do this for you if you believe in Him; you will be blessed with great peace, knowing that everything will be okay. As Jesus slept in the ship and a great storm came, the disciples became worried and afraid. They did not have peace among themselves; they allowed fear to take over their spirits. God rose and rebuked the wind and spoke three words to the sea: "Peace, be still," and immediately the water calmed and He gave the disciples rest (Matthew 4:39).

Jesus has already given us His peace. John 14:27 says, "Peace I leave with you, my peace I give unto you: not as the world giveth, give I unto you. Let not your heart be troubled, neither let it be afraid." The peace of God is another gift to us. I ask that you internalize the Scripture and feel the gift of peace in your heart, the calming to your spirit.

Can you imagine the peace Jesus felt when He rose on the third day and ascended into heaven to be with His Father? All trials from His cup of life, tribulations, and crucifixion for the redemption of our sins and pain disappeared immediately when He said, "It is finished" (John 19:30). The comfort and magnificent love, light, and radiance of His glory upon His arrival in heaven, I cannot imagine a more greater peace than the peace Christ must have felt after completing God's will and fulfilling the Scriptures.

Second Corinthians 13:11 says, "Finally, brethren, farewell. Be perfect, be of good comfort, be of one mind, live in peace; and the God of love and peace shall be with you."

The peace I feel with God in my life.

Long-Suffering

> But thou, O Lord, art a God full of
> compassion, and gracious, longsuffering,
> and plenteous in mercy and truth.
> —Psalm 86:15

> Howbeit for this cause I obtained mercy,
> that in me first Jesus Christ might show forth all
> longsuffering, for a pattern to them which should
> hereafter believe on him to life everlasting.
> —1 Timothy 1:16

> But thou hast fully known my doctrine, manner of
> life, purpose, faith, longsuffering, charity, patience,
> persecutions, afflictions, which came unto me at
> Antioch, at Iconium at Lystra; what persecutions I
> endured: but out of them all the Lord delivered me.
> —2 Timothy 3:10

How can we compare our lives today to Jesus and his long-suffering? Jesus as a child left His Mother, Mary, and father, Joseph, to be about His Father God's business. Jesus followed His Father's will by traveling the road to Calvary knowing what was ahead of Him and giving His life for our sins so that we may have eternal life with God. Jesus was stripped and whipped with hatred tearing into His flesh with each blow. He was pierced in His sides with swords, mocked, ridiculed, and a crown of thorns was placed on His head, pressing through His flesh until the bones of Jesus's skull stopped the penetration, making the blood of Jesus stream down His face and giving the appearance of red tears—tears of blood. Jesus Christ shed His blood for our sins.

    Christ carried the cup of crucifixion and long-suffering with our salvation in His heart. Christ endured until He gave up the Ghost on Golgotha Hill, the place of the skull. Jesus was hanging from the support of His palms; His flesh was tearing because of the weight of His body and the gravity's pull. Can you imagine the heaviness of Christ's body on His hands and feet, the pain and long-suffering Christ had to endure? Christ's entire body's weight was pulling down on His hands as He hung, and the force was pressing down on His nailed feet with the weight of His entire body pushing down on the immovable nails. Unlike the nails we see today made with modern factory precision and technology of smoothness and sharp tips designed for easy penetration, I imagine the nails used on Christ were very large, imperfect with jagged edges and wide uneven sides with blunt tips. Can you imagine hearing the clanging sound from the pounding force of the hammer needed for the nails to penetrate Christ's hands, feet, and the wood that held Jesus on the cross? The hammer was clanging loudly as it hit the nail with each blow over and over again. Jesus suffered for us on Calvary. Jesus stayed on the cross, He did not come down, and I have described to you the true meaning of long-suffering. Can you compare your suffering to the long-suffering of Christ? The answer to that question should be no, we cannot compare ourselves to Jesus nor to His pain. Jesus had to fulfill the Scriptures and obey God's will. Christ knew of the long-suffering He would have to endure. That is why He was praying to God in the garden of Gethsemane, asking God to take the cup away from Him if it was God's will.

    Although you may not think so, the spirit of long-suffering is much easier for us in today's world. The crosses that we may bear are sometimes of our own creation when we take matters into our own hands without seeking and asking God if it is His will. If it is not God's will, your cross may be imperfect without God's blessings. In comparison, can you imagine the effects of your cross with God's blessings? If you believe you are suffering and you are not doing God's will, your long-suffering may be the work of the adversary attempting to steal your joy. John 10:10 says, "The thief cometh not, but for to steal, and to kill, and to destroy: I am come that they might have life, and that they might have it more abundantly." If God has handed you a cross of long-suffering and you take it up and do His will, your long-suffering will be followed with blessings from God because He loves you.

I never imagined the day when I would feel like I was suffering or bearing my cross. God has always taken care of me and blessed me in many ways even when I did not realize that I was being blessed. I believe my long-suffering is happening in my life now. Caring for my mother is my cross to bear; she has dementia. I will not discuss my experiences dealing with her dementia out of love and respect for my mother; however, I will tell you about some of the effects her dementia had on me. I have cried many days and fought back many tears. I even became depressed and threatened to quit caring for her and move. I have driven around many nights with no place to go then return home to face another night and day of the same hurt and pain. I asked my husband, "How did I get into this situation?" His response was "You are doing God's will."

When I think about it, my mother came to me one day and said that it was time for her to go to a nursing home. My inner spirit told me to tell her "No, I will take care of you." Others told me not to do it because it is not easy. I did not listen to outside voices; I listened to my spirit.

I remain with my mother today, carrying my cross and laying down my life, as I once knew it because of my love for her. I now realize that long-suffering comes when you truly love someone. I understand that she is the cross that I must bear. In comparison, Mom to me is like we are to Christ; we are the cause of Christ's long-suffering and the cross He had to bear. Christ endured because He loves us. She does not realize the pain and sacrifices that I am going through to care for her, and she will never understand or appreciate it because of her condition. That is how we are to Christ. We will never truly know the pain and suffering that Jesus has gone through carrying the cross for our salvation; we can only imagine it. I am still carrying my cross because I believe it is God's will. I don't want to paint this perfect picture of myself because I have complained to my siblings when they will listen, then I feel convicted because I am not behaving Christlike when I complain, so I pray and ask God to give me strength to continue.

My siblings believe that I am in emotional pain, but that does not change my situation. I am given a break once in a while, and my cross is carried by a sibling in the same manner of care for my mother but only for a very brief time, and the cross is returned to me, which reminds me of this scripture, Matthew 27:32, which says, "And as they came out, they found a man of Cyrene, Simon by name: him they compelled to bear His cross." Although Simon helped to carry the cross for Jesus, he did not endure long-suffering for Him. The long-suffering of crucifixion was for Jesus alone because the Scripture had to be fulfilled, and it was God's will. We should realize that our long-suffering is not the same as Christ's; our long-suffering is mild and most often than not caused by our own decisions made without asking God if it is His will.

I would like for you to recognize your cross and find the love in the long-suffering of your cross bearing, and write it in the next two pages as a reminder to yourself and as a reminder of the cross that Christ had to bear for you.

Understanding that your long-suffering is mild in comparison to Christ's pain and sacrifice, your scriptural reflections of the crucifixion of Jesus will help you to endure your cross with love and long-suffering in your heart. Luke 9:23 says, "And He said to them all, if any man will come after me, let him deny himself, and take up his cross daily, and follow me." Follow Christ, and endure your cross, whatever it may be. Your reward will be great in the kingdom of heaven. It is my love for Christ and the Holy Word of God that is giving me strength to continue to carry my cross. My long-suffering is in remembrance of Jesus Christ, my Lord and Savior.

LADWYINA TOLAR-SLATER

My cross to bear and the long-suffering that comes with it because I love.

Gentleness

> But the wisdom that is from above is first pure,
> then peaceable, gentle, and easy to be entreated,
> full of mercy and good fruits, without.
> —James 3:17

> To speak evil of no man, to be no brawlers, but
> gentle. Showing all meekness unto all men.
> —Titus 3:2

> And the servant of the Lord must not strive; but be
> gentle unto all men, apt to teach, patient.
> —Timothy 2:24

What does it mean to be gentle? I believe almost everyone in the world had been gentle in his or her lifetime, regardless if others recognize it. If you have ever cradled a newborn baby in your arms, maybe the mother or father of the child gave care to show you how to hold the baby's head gently with no abrupt movements to startle him or her, how to speak softly to them, and how to rock them gently. This is how God has been gentle with us. Have you ever cried yourself to sleep and when you awoke, you felt a little better after resting? It was the Comforter that God sent you to give you peace, dry your tears, and allow you to fall asleep and rest gently.

God's will for us is to be gentle with everyone we come in contact with. A perfect example was when Jesus reattached the ear unto the high priest's servant Malchus after Simon Peter smote it with his sword (Luke 22:50–51). By reattaching Malchus's ear, Jesus was teaching Peter to have mercy while being gentle to all men, including Malchus, even though he was one of the many that participated in the arrest of Jesus (Titus 3:2). There are so many temptations cast before us in life; it is very important that you recognize them and remember that God will not tempt us to act in an ungodly manner. That type of behavior is a dark spirit (James 1:13).

Christ wants us to become gentle with everyone. The spirit gentleness is a reflection of His kindness, patience, compassion, and concern. I am actively walking daily in the spirit of gentleness. I am the guardian of my teenage granddaughter who is very fragile in spirit because of the death of her mother and my daughter. It has been a trying three years with lots of emotions and grieving coming from both my granddaughter and myself. I never dreamed that I would lose my daughter at a young age and become the guardian to my granddaughter who never dreamed of losing her mother at the age of twelve. From day one, I hid my tears from my granddaughter because I didn't want her to see my pain because she had her own pain and loss to deal with. I have shown her love, patience, and gentleness with every fiber of my being while being a servant to her and to the Lord. As I compose this, my eyes still overflow with tears and my heart with the sympathy that I feel for my granddaughter because I cannot imagine myself being a child without a mother although I truly believe that it would not have been easy. I have accepted the fact that after caring for my granddaughter, no matter how hard I try to ease her pain, my spirit of gentleness is not the only spirit needed to comfort her. All the fruit of the Spirit are needed, and I have asked God in a quiet way to increase within me and allow me to decrease in the spirit that want me to chastise her with anger when she acts out in an unkind manner. I am not perfect and have been caught off guard by her anger, causing me at times to become that same type of angry spirit. That is when I begin to pray and ask God to help me through this storm, and to be honest, I have actually counted the number of years until she is off to college. She is a good girl and will later approach me with a better spirit, letting me know without saying that she is sorry. I understand and forgive her.

I thank God for being an example of how to practice all the fruit of the Spirit. I believe the gentleness that I have learned from my Mentor, Christ, is carrying us through the storm. One of my siblings mentioned to me, "I don't know if you know this, but you are not the same person that you use to be." My response to her was "I do know that I have changed." I have never been a bad person. My sister may not understand that I was once blind, but now I see with the spiritual light that radiates from Christ.

LADWYINA TOLAR-SLATER

These are my reflections of gentleness that I give to others in my life.

Goodness

He hath shewed thee, O man, what is good; and what doth the Lord require of thee, but to do justly, and to love mercy, and to walk humbly with thy God?
—Micah 6:8

A good man out of the good treasure of the heart bringeth forth good things: and an evil man out of the evil treasure bringeth forth evil things.
—Matthew 12:35

As we have therefore opportunity, let us do good unto all men, especially unto them who are of the household of faith.
—Galatians 6:10

The goodness of Christ can be described as a complex compound consisting of every divine essence within Him, from the crown of His head to the soles of His feet. Every aspect of Christ's goodness shined through as He taught the disciples in prayers, parables, and sermons, also with His many miraculous works. Christ walked in the spirit of goodness; He spoke in the spirit of goodness and gave up His Ghost in the spirit of goodness.

Unconditional is the type of goodness that is required of everyone that want to be Christlike and walk with Him in the spirit of goodness. Your walk, talk, and action of goodness have to be honest and do not envy nor strive to receive rewards because of your acts of goodness. Jesus spoke to His disciples and the multitude of people to put the treasure of goodness into their hearts and concern in their minds to prepare them to spread the spirit of goodness (Matthew 12:35). We must understand God's goodness and become an example of His goodness by showing others through our actions.

The goodness that you give must come from the heart with true meaning. Something as simple as a compliment to someone can be tainted, stripped of goodness, if it is not coming from the goodness of the heart. For example, a compliment can be given to someone regarding the dress she is wearing and then followed up with a comment saying, "Thank goodness, she stopped wearing the other dress." The compliment was not out of pure goodness because in the same breath, it was destroyed with the judging comments regarding a different dress previously worn. Grasp purity and honesty, and hold onto it tightly; it is a portion of the complex compounds in the essence of Christ's goodness. When you are able to mimic what you perceive to be the goodness that Christ possesses, then you will have gained a fraction of His goodness. Consider the scripture found in Matthew 7:12: "Therefore all things whatsoever ye would that men should do to you, do ye even so to them: for this is the law and the prophets." Consider giving copious amounts of goodness to everyone you come in contact with. Can you imagine the goodness you would receive in return if everyone practiced giving the spirit of God's goodness? The goodness of Christ can be found throughout the Bible. He has left us many examples of how we should behave and how to show goodness to others while we walk this earth.

Use the following pages to write about how you have mirrored God's goodness after you have examined yourself. If you have fallen short, remind yourself of what you should be doing in terms of goodness to become more Christlike.

BEAUTIFUL FOR CHRIST

This is my spirit of goodness that I have shared with others unconditionally.

Faith

Therefore being justified by faith, we have peace with
God through our Lord Jesus Christ: By whom also
we have access by faith into this grace wherein we
stand, and rejoice in hope of the glory of God.
—Romans 5:1–2

Now faith is the substance of things hoped
for, the evidence of things not seen.
—Hebrews 11:1

But without faith it is impossible to please Him: for he
that cometh to God must believe that He is, and that
He is a rewarder of them that diligently seek Him.
—Hebrews 11:6

The faith within your heart, mind, and soul is the manifestation of belief without a doubt that God, Jesus, and the Holy Spirit are all Power and the Rewarder to those who diligently seek Him (Hebrew 11:6). Faith in the Holy Trinity and the Holy Scripture is important for studying and understanding God's doctrine that provides instructions, corrections, and guidance toward righteousness (2 Timothy 3:16). Faith is what leads us to the acceptance of God and our salvation. We cannot have faith in God and not have faith in the Trinity.

There are many scriptures and miracles in the Bible regarding faith. There was the woman with the issue of blood. I am certain in the days of Christ that she did not know what the issue was or what may have caused it. She only knew that she had been suffering for twelve years with no cure available from the physicians. Her faith in Jesus was so great that she knew if she could touch His garment, she would be healed. Faith is the substance of things hoped for (Hebrews 11:1). She had the faith the size of a mustard seed, and her mountain to move was her issue of blood. She believed that she would be healed because of her faith in Jesus. With the throng around Him, it was difficult for her to reach Jesus. Because of her unbreakable faith in Jesus, she was determined to be near Him by pushing her way through the multitude of people and the disciples; she came up behind him and touched the border of His garment. After touching His garment, Jesus knew He had been touched, and the virtue had been released from Him.

What we must realize is the unwavering divine faith that Christ has in God, that faith gave Jesus the ability to perform miracles here on earth. For that reason, the woman was immediately healed; she no longer had the issue of blood. She fell down before Jesus and explained why she had touched Him, and Jesus spoke to her, "And He said unto her Daughter, be of good comfort: thy faith hath made thee whole; go in peace" (Luke 8:48).

Because of her faith, she rejoiced in the glory of God (Romans 5:1–2).

The miracle the lady with the issue of blood received from Jesus was because she maintained unbreakable faith in Jesus and because of Christ's unbreakable faith in God. No one could stop her or convince her to change her mind; she possessed a passion for Jesus that was so unshakable; no one could take her faith away. That is the type of faith that we must have and protect and cultivate. Unfortunate circumstances may happen to us in our cup of life, but we must maintain the faith the size of mustard seed, and we also can move mountains. A mustard seed is so small. If dropped, it can become lost and never be found. Don't drop it. Place it deep in your heart and soul where it can grow into a passion so great it will become inseparable and, as Jesus said, "Daughter, thy faith hath made the whole" (Mark 5:34). With faith comes trusting in the Lord in all that you do. If it is God's will, you will not fail. Without faith, it is impossible to please God (Hebrew 11:6).

To move a mountain may seem impossible to you because it is so enormous. You must remember that you are not moving the mountain; God is. Nothing is too large for God to handle. You need great faith. He sees all and knows all. The mountain that you are trying to move, if it is not God's will to move, it will remain. The message from God may tell you to change directions, turn, and go around the mountain in a different direction to move it. Pray and ask God to show you the way, and when He answers, listen to your Holy Spirit, hear Him, and obey His will; and the mountain that you thought was in your way is no longer there. Remember, all good and pure thoughts come from God. Have unbreakable, unshakable, and inseparable faith in God, and He will show you how to move your mountain.

What my unbreakable, unshakable, inseparable faith in God means to me.

Meekness

Blessed are the meek for they shall inherit the earth.
—Matthew 5:5

Take my yoke upon you, and learn of me; for I am meek and lowly in heart and ye shall find rest unto your souls.
—Matthew 11:29

But sanctify the Lord God in your hearts: and be ready always to give an answer to every man that asketh you a reason of the hope that is in you with meekness and fear.
—1 Peter 3:5

One of the divine Spirits of Jesus is meekness, and the Bible speaks of becoming Christlike. Jesus said, "Take my yoke upon you and learn from me" (Matthew 11:29). A yoke is a device placed and locked upon the necks of two adjacent oxen, joining them together for controlling the oxen while they work together. By using the yoke method, the oxen are stronger while walking and working together down the same path at the same pace for completing the designated task. Jesus has used the yoke as a symbol, letting you know that He will be by your side guiding, teaching, and working with you if you allow Him. The strength of God will guide you to the spirit of meekness. If you remain connected to Him, your soul will find rest.

While yoked, you can follow and mirror the meekness and lowly heart of Jesus; you will find peace with Him as you become humbled while learning beside Christ. Jesus will teach you by counsel from the Holy Spirit, giving you understanding of how to handle your burdens with meekness. Christ knows all about your needs and how to make your burdens light. Walk with Him, and wait upon the Lord. Allow the yoke of Christ to guide you while keeping the same meek spirit as Christ. You will endure all things gracefully by the grace of God. Become yoked with Christ; allow Him to hold your hand while remaining meek and humbled in heart. Jesus will guide you and bless you with His teachings. Become Christlike, and know that you can inherit the earth with Jesus by your side, and praise God in your heart. Your cup of life has the sweetener of Christ added to it. When you drink from it, remember Christ and pray that His meekness reside within you so that one day, you may be blessed in a mighty way and inherit the earth (Matthew 5:5).

LADWYINA TOLAR-SLATER

Your prayer: ask God to allow you to become beautiful for Christ by gifting you with all the fruit and gifts of the Spirit.

Temperance

> This I say then, walk in the Spirit and ye
> shall not fulfill the lust of the flesh.
> —Galatians 5:16

> But put ye on the Lord Jesus Christ, and make not
> provision for the flesh, to fulfill the lusts thereof.
> —Romans 13:14

> And to knowledge temperance; and to temperance
> patience; and to patience Godliness.
> —2 Peter 1:6

The meaning of temperance is to approach an action, thought, or feeling with moderation of restraint while bringing about balance. Several examples came to mind. My first thought was of tempering chocolate by controlling the temperature. Chocolate is melted, causing the molecules in the chocolate to become loose and unconforming or confused. By adding new cooled chocolate to the melted chocolate using moderation and restraint from attempting to hurry the cooling process of the blended, melted chocolate, you will be able to give the tempered chocolate a new form of your choice as it cools to give that beautiful shine, that delicious chocolaty flavor, and the perfect texture that melts in your mouth.

My second thought was of the statue Lady Justice. You may have seen her in in the lobby of a court building or, in passing, in front of the court or on the grounds nearby. Lady Justice represents the moral force of the judicial system, promising fairness. Her attributes are the blindfold that covers her eyes representing impartiality, promising that justice will be applied without regard to wealth, power, or status; the balance she is holding that symbolizes the weighing of evidence, fairly measuring the strengths of a case's support and opposition; and lastly, the sword in her other hand representing enforcement and respect. Collectively, the symbolization of Lady Justice and the office of the jurisdiction of the judge and jury that is meticulously selected brings about temperance by blending moral forces together with justice and mercy, thereby ensuring a fair sentence for the crime accused of.

The absence of temperance in actuality can be recognized by acknowledging that we the people are flesh and of the world because God has placed the world in our hearts. To temper ourselves so that we may not be devoured by the world, we must bring Jesus into our lives. Christ is the Lamp to our feet showing us the way, along with the Holy Spirit convicting our consciousness to make righteous and wise decisions. If we are obedient to the Holy Spirit, we will be able to approach life in moderation and restraint. The spirit of temperance that is required of you is of God's Spirit.

The power of Jesus is mighty so much so that He tempered the scribes and Pharisees while becoming the Judge and Jury without the crowd knowing. When Jesus began writing with His finger on the ground, Christ asked, "For those of you without sin, cast the first stone." Christ was tempering the crowd; they were very hot like the chocolate with anger. That one question Jesus asked placed a spirit of thought and conviction into the minds of the sinners in the crowd. Because God is omniscient, all knowing, He knew there were many guilty accusers among them. Maybe even the other party to the adultery that the woman was accused of may have also been in the crowd, anxiously judging and issuing a verdict of guilty without a trial because of the lack of the spirit of temperance within him or her.

The angry crowd was prepared to carry out a sentence of stoning the accused to death. Jesus stood among the crowd of hot, melted, and confused chocolate as the cool and calm Chocolate with the spirit of temperance, and with moderation, Christ made one profound statement while using restraint from acknowledging the crowd's anger. He said, "He that is without sin among you, let him first cast a stone at her" (John 8:7). Christ's Spirit of temperance calmed the crowd by placing restraint and conviction in their hearts while reminding them that the lady was not the only one that had sinned. Christ brought to light that they, the members of the crowd, who complained were not righteous and without sin by calmly making a statement, bringing forward the convictions in their hearts. Jesus recognized the judgment of the crowd, but Christ's Spirit was working and tempering the chocolate with His Spirit, then one by one, they left without stoning her. Christ executed the jurisdiction of the judge and brought the symbols of Lady Justice into fruition.

Romans 13:14 says, "But put ye on the Lord Jesus Christ, and make not provision for the flesh, to fulfill the lusts thereof."

The scripture tells us how we should live our lives, not catering to the flesh; too much of anything other than God is not good for you. We must become cognizant of how we blend or mix our lives with the world because the results of our actions, whatever they may be, will have an impact on yourself and the lives of others.

The temperance that the Holy Bible is speaking of is of restraint and moderation of the consumption of alcoholic beverages; however, we should consider broadening the spectrum because of the world today to include moderation of many vices of the world, such as overeating, smoking, gambling, and partying, to name a few of the innumerable vices. There are of course a few other vices that I will mention; however, in my opinion, the vices should be eliminated altogether. Therefore, I will only mention them, and they are the following: arrogance, greed, envy, anger, lust, gluttony, and laziness. Temperance is self-control in your actions, becoming the opposite of negative forces of the vices while becoming complementary in all that you do. Jesus showed temperance while here on earth. We, the people of the world, should walk with Christ in an attempt to emulate His beautiful Spirit of temperance while denying the lust of the flesh (Galatians 5:16).

LADWYINA TOLAR-SLATER

Changes I should make in my life to gain temperance.

PART 6

THE ADVERSARY, SATAN

Recognizing Satan

And the great dragon was cast out, the old serpent,
called the Devil, and Satan, which deceiveth
the whole world: he was cast out into the earth,
and his angels were cast out with him.
—Revelation 12:9

Be sober, be vigilant, because your adversary the devil, as a roaring lion, walketh about, seeking whom he may devour.
—1 Peter 5:8

He that committeth sin is of the devil; for the devil sinneth from the beginning. For this purpose the Son of God was manifested that he might destroy the works of the devil.
—1 John 3:8

I must inform you that it disturbs me to include this section because I do not want to give any acknowledgment to Satan; however, I must speak of him because it is important for you to know that Satan is your enemy. Satan will not be happy that you have given your life to Christ. Be aware that he may tempt you to sin in any way that is against God's will. Satan works against God and His doctrine. He is jealous and envious of God. Satan is the ruler of darkness and of all evil principalities of the world. He is the ruler of wickedness and is here to devour anyone that will allow him (1 Peter 5:8). I say allow because you can resist him in the name of Jesus. Satan is a deceiver to those that have not accepted God and can appear as an angel of light.

Satan, also known as the devil, has angels of darkness that were cast out of heaven with him. The great dragon is here on earth to deceive the world (Revelation 12:9). There are many people in the world that do not understand that they are allowing Satan's spirit to work within them. There was a time when I thought I should fight my battles by arguing to defend myself, and when the argument was over, I did not feel any better. I have grown in Christ and learned to walk away from many arguments, allowing the other person to have the last word. I will admit that holding my tongue is hard when someone is provoking me. I have learned by listening to the Holy Spirit on how to hold my tongue, and I promised myself to let it go and give it to God because He will fight my battles.

Satan controls the spirit of a liar, murderer, thief, whoremonger, and every spirit against God's teachings. Satan is here roaming the earth to devour every good spirit within you if you allow it to happen. He wants your soul for his own to control after the judgment. Satan attempted to bribe Jesus with control of all the kingdoms of the world and their glory if Christ would fall down and worship him (Matthew 4:1–11). It is important that you learn how to recognize an evil spirit and pray for God's protection.

Where are the evil spirits? Look around the world, and listen to the news. You will hear of robberies, murders, molestations, lies, and anything of that horrible nature. Those offenses are the works of Satan's evil spirits. An evil spirit will provoke you and will attempt to make you break God's Ten Commandments and the commandments that Jesus gave us. An evil spirit is one that wants you to question if God is real. As God has blessed you, Satan will place stumbling blocks in your way and blinders over your eyes in an attempt to keep you from knowing that you are blessed and that God is with you. Satan is not happy when another person has given their life to Christ, and it is the job of Satan's angels to tempt the Christian, causing he or she to fall back into the world of sin.

Pray constantly in Jesus's name, asking God to cover and protect you and your family from all the wiles of Satan's evil spirits, including temptation, hurt, harm, and danger while wearing the whole armor of God so that you will be able to stand with Jesus against evil. Remain sober and vigilant while submitting yourself to God and resisting the devil, and you must know that the closer you become to God, the more Satan will attempt to touch or interfere with your life in Christ. Satan will try to steal your joy. Allow the Holy Spirit to guide you with pure and good decisions from God.

Have you ever had a dream that was so bad that you decided to call it a nightmare? The worst things that you could imagine was happening to you, and upon awaking, you realized that it was a bad dream. That was Satan trying to steal your joy while you were sleeping. Rebuke him in your dream in Jesus's name, and the dream will change. Upon awaking, do not react to the bad dreams in a negative way; that is what he wants you to do. Thank God for waking you and clothing you in your right mind, giving you the ability to realize that you were dreaming. When you have God on your side during your consciousness, Satan cannot touch you with God's loving arms of protection around you. Pray before going to sleep, bring God into your mind and heart, ask for forgiveness and protection, and you will have a beautiful peaceful rest. Resist Satan and call on Jesus, and Satan will flee. James 4:7 says, "Submit yourselves therefore to God. Resist the devil, and he will flee from you."

I discussed the full armor of God earlier. I would be amiss if I did not discuss with you the scripture (1 Peter 1:13). The scripture is telling me to prepare my mind, the prefrontal cortex, located near the front of the brain, for battle. Satan, when he strikes, he attacks the mind. This is possible when we let our guards down or are not girded up with the protection of God. You ask, how do we protect ourselves from Satan? Pray and ask for God's protection, and believe that God is with you. We can ensure that our temple is strong in the Holy Spirit by sanctifying ourselves by asking for sanctification and receiving the blessings from Christ Jesus. A holy temple possesses an element of sobriety among many other elements of purity with the bonding and abiding in the Holy Spirit and with unbreakable faith covered by God's precious blood and His hedge of protection surrounding you with a promise of grace at the revelation of our Lord Jesus Christ! God has given us the scriptural procedures that we should follow to become beautiful for Christ.

LADWYINA TOLAR-SLATER

These are my habits that I choose to release from my spirit to make Satan flee from me, in the name of Jesus, I pray.

PART 7

BEAUTIFUL FOR CHRIST

Scriptural Procedures to Becoming Beautiful for Christ

Put on therefore, as the elect of God, holy and beloved, bowels of mercies, kindness, humbleness of mind, meekness, longsuffering. Forbearing one another and forgiving one another, if any man have a quarrel against any: even as Christ forgave you, so also do ye. And above all these things put on charity, which is the bond of perfectness. And let the peace of God rule in your hearts, to which also ye are called in one body; and be ye thankful. Let the word of Christ dwell in you richly in all wisdom, teaching and admonishing one another in psalms and hymns and spiritual songs, singing with grace in your hearts to the Lord. And whatsoever ye do in word or deed, do all in the name of the Lord Jesus, giving thanks to God and the Father by him.
—Colossians 3:12–17

Finally, brethren, whatsoever things are true, whatsoever things are honest, whatsoever things are just, whatsoever things are pure, whatsoever things are lovely, whatsoever things are of good report; if there be any virtue, and if there be any praise think on these things.
—Philippians 4:8

O Worship the Lord in the beauty of
Holiness fear before Him, all the earth.
—Psalm 96:9

Your passion to study God's Holy Word should be like a fire shut up in your bones growing bigger and brighter with eagerness to understand and learn how to walk in the light while worshipping God in the beauty of holiness. Embrace your revelations, and share the good news about the Gospel of peace with those who will listen. Become beautiful for Christ and a blessing to all.

Beauty is a phenomenon that God created. We should understand and accept it because God said, "Let us make man in our image, after our likeness" (Genesis 1:26). I ask, is God beautiful? Beauty is found within your innermost being; it is your love for God that is within your temple—your heart, mind, and soul; it is your relationship with and love for Christ. Beauty is the conversations you share with God, praising His holy name; it is the love and blessings that you give to your neighbors; it is the shining light projected by you so that others may see the good works you have done, in the name of Jesus, that is pleasing to God and an example to all men and women that love God and an example to those that may not know Him. It is the walks that you take with God every day and the moments you share with Him, opening up your heart, giving Him all your concerns when your cup of life's events that happen are not happy ones. It is when you tell God, "I accept Your will." Beauty is when you recognize and hear the Holy Spirit's voice speaking to you.

Beautiful for Christ is when you are not angry with God and understand that you could never be angry with Him. It is when you remember a scripture after hearing bad news and the Holy Spirit whispers in your ears, telling you to trust in the Lord, and you say, "Yes, Lord, I hear and trust You." To become beautiful for Christ and carry the essence of God's light, love God, resist the devil, become Christlike, speak kind words, follow God's commandments and His will, walk in the light, and praise and glorify God in all that you do. Pray and repent daily, asking for forgiveness, and last but not the least, allow your beautiful appearance, your light, to shine before Jesus Christ. Yes, beautiful is God, and we are made in His image. Take hold of this statement, and believe it. God does not create anyone less than beautiful. We can never thank God enough because of the infinite blessings that He has and will continue to bestow upon us. God is so magnificent that praising Him will forever be on my lips here on earth and in the kingdom of heaven.

BEAUTIFUL FOR CHRIST

Write a beautiful heartfelt letter to God.

Walking in the Beauty of Holiness

And thine ears shall hear a word behind thee saying,
this is the way, walk ye in it, when ye turn to the
right hand, and when ye turn to the left.
—Isaiah 30:21

But he that is joined unto the Lord is one spirit.
—1 Corinthians 6:17

This I say then, walk in the Spirit and ye
shall not fulfill the lust of the flesh.
—Galatians 5:16

Arise, shine, for thy light is come, and the
glory of the Lord is risen upon thee.
—Isaiah 60:1

Walking in the flesh is a normal function of mobility, as we know it. We alternately place one foot forward at a time. However, when you are walking in the spirit of light, God is with you as one Spirit (1 Corinthians 6:17). Christ's walk is with glory and honor and all the divine essence within Him. Put yourself in the shoes of His disciples when they were walking with Christ. They did not know how to walk with Christ in the Spirit, but they learned by laying down their worldly ways and denying the flesh, then they walked in the Spirit as Christ taught them.

Think of it as being on the job training. You will learn, as you work toward perfection, in the beauty of holiness. I can only imagine what it would have been like walking with Christ. In today's world, it has become harder to draw people to Christ. Jesus would not be looking for people that have already accepted Him as their Lord and Savior. Jesus would be preaching in parables and teaching those that have gone astray and those that have not accepted Him. God would teach those who will listen about the fruit of the Spirit; how to walk in the light and to love one another. Jesus would focus on anyone that is not abiding in God's word by planting seeds into the minds of those who may not know Him and into the hearts of those who may have forgotten Him and gone astray.

Do you recall that I asked you to picture yourself in the shoes of His disciples? You would be there near Jesus's side trying to bring lost sheep to Him to become saved or healed. Your light will be shining brightly with truth and love. But sometimes, our light may become dim. Jesus would correct us with His actions and teach us that we should not judge others and to help those that are in need and to feed those that are hungry and to give to those that do not have. Jesus would teach us that it is better to give than to receive. Think about it, would you rather be the person in need, hoping that someone will bless you, or the person that have to give and can bless others? He would tell us to give our riches to those that are in need and follow Him. Jesus would teach us not to judge unless we want to be judged. Christ would tell us to respect ourselves, make peace with our brothers, and love our neighbors.

Walking in the light with Jesus is about obeying God's commandments, allowing God's will to be done, to love and not hate, make peace, not war, to speak the truth, walk by faith, live righteously, and testify the goodness of Christ. Your ears will hear the Spirit speaking to you, letting you know that this is the way (Isaiah 30:21). The light of Jesus is the way, which are the truth, love, and righteousness. We are all created equal with one salvation and one name in heaven. To walk in the light with Christ, we must keep in mind what Jesus was doing while He was here on earth. He is our Mentor and an example of how we should live while we are here. All of our walks must be acceptable in the sight of God and a perfect example to those around us. Matthew 5:48 says, "Be ye therefore perfect, even as your Father which is in heaven is perfect." When you evaluate yourself and recognize a reflection of Christ's love and truth within you and others can see it also, that is a way of knowing your light is shining brightly and you are beautiful for Christ. With that being said, most importantly, Christ will acknowledge you before His Father.

Several years ago, the doorbell rang in my place of business. I immediately answered it. There was an unknown man standing in the doorway. I welcomed him to come in. After speaking with him, I learned, to my understanding, that he did not have a reason for ringing the bell. He entered the funeral home and made pleasant small talk. I was courteous, polite, and patient with him; I learned that it was not an emergency, and that no one had passed away. He gave no reason for wanting to speak to me, but before his departure, he turned and looked at me as he exited and said that he could see my light shining. When I think about that experience, it brought the following scripture to my memory, Matthew 5:16, which says, "Let your light so shine before men, that they may see your good works, and glorify your Father which is in heaven."

I will never forget that encounter, and I sometimes wonder, was he one of God's angels? The Bible speaks of the possibility of us entertaining angels unknowingly. Hebrews 13:2 tells us, "Be not forgetful to entertain strangers: for thereby some have entertained angels unawares." I could have been curt with him once I realized he had no business with me and also he had no explanation as to why he rang the bell. Instead, I treated the gentleman with kindness until he was ready to depart. Now when I think of him, I realize that he was very kind and his light was shining also. Maybe he was an angel delivering a message to me to continue walking in the beauty of holiness by following the beautiful essence of Christ. This is what we strive for: to embrace and become beautiful for Christ by walking in the beauty of holiness.

Reflections of how I am walking in the beauty of holiness.

Allow Your Light to Shine

For God, who commanded the light to shine out of darkness, has shined in our hearts, to give the light of the knowledge of the glory of God in the face of Jesus Christ.
—2 Corinthians 4:6

Ye are the light of the world. A city that is set on an hill cannot be hid.
—Matthew 5:14

Allow your light to shine by walking in the Spirit of God. God's light is so brilliantly bright in comparison to the fraction of glimmer that we may project. Can you imagine what the world would be like if everyone you came in contact with carried that shining glimmer from the light of Christ? The entire world would be shining brightly like the moon and the sun; the only difference would be the love that would be felt by everyone receiving the light. The kind gestures given to someone that you do not know will be remembered in their hearts because of your glimmer of light shining. Your goal is to impact someone's life positively, letting him or her know by your actions and works that God is here with us and that He loves us all. Know that your light is a reflection of God's love, and it must always be on and never hidden for as long as you have breath. Remember, while you are in Christ, you are the light of the world that cannot be hidden (Matthew 5:14). Your light shining can be as simple as holding the door for someone or running errands for the elderly or cleaning their homes. If you have it to give and it has been asked of you, then give. We are here to be a blessing to others and to show God's love in every way.

I attended a track meet at the University of Notre Dame. My daughter Brittany was competing for Michigan State. While my family and I were waiting to see Brittany before our departure, I noticed a student lying on the floor in the doorway, and everyone was walking by and stepping over her without concern. I was immediately alarmed and needed to find out if she was okay. I was thinking that if she were my child, I would want someone to check to ensure that she was okay. I walked over and stooped down to see if she was conscious and breathing. After speaking with her and asking if she needed help, she assured me that she was fine. I believe that is an example of allowing God's light to shine. She may have felt my glimmer of light in her heart and now believe someone cared. It did not take much effort on my part to do a wellness check; we as followers of Christ must show love, concern, and care.

Because we are humans, we may find that our light has become dim or may flicker sometimes like a light bulb burning out. What should we do to troubleshoot or repair the flickering light? We check to see if the cord is completely plugged into the outlet, and we also check the bulb to see if it is completely screwed into the socket. That is how we handle a flickering light bulb. What should we do when we feel that our light has become dim and begun to flicker? We should turn to God's Holy Word to refresh our studies to revive our spirit in Christ. Ask your family, friends, and pastor to pray for you, and you pray fervently for yourself. Ask God to give you strength to resist the wiles of the world. Continue to pray and trust in the Lord. He will renew your strength, turning your flicker into a shining light again. God's love is our example on how we should let our light shine. We should pray and ask God to give us strength to continue with our walk with Him. You must continue to study because you are faced with new challenges every day in your cup of life. By studying, you will find the answers to those challenges. The book of Proverbs contains many answers regarding life's challenges in general, and if adhered to, the knowledge you gain may prevent mistakes and regrets from being made in the future.

Start your day by giving thanks and praises to God for waking you up and giving you health, strength, and a sound mind. Ask God to bless your day, and let His will be done. Also ask God to order your steps, to lead and guide your thoughts, actions, and speech; ask God to cover you with His precious blood by keeping you from any hurt, harm, and danger. When you go out into the world, you do not know what you will be confronted with, and for that reason, you should pray and ask God to bless those that you come in contact with, including your family, friends, coworkers, and strangers. By asking God to bless everyone that you come in contact with, you will have prayed for them, and God will take care so that all will be well with you and whoever you come in contact with. Also ask God to give you traveling grace as you go about your day.

Because Satan is busy, he will try to extinguish your shining light, like blowing out a candle. Be aware of those you come in contact with, and recognize if they are walking in the light with Christ or if they are walking in darkness. If you come in contact with someone that has road rage while driving, let your light shine, and do not engage in Satan's fight. Give a silent prayer for them by asking God to guide them safely down the highway or street; this will protect another driver from Satan's angry road rage ways.

Galatians 5:16 says, "This I say then, walk in the Spirit, and ye shall not fulfill the lust of the flesh."

Take a moment to internalize what the above scripture is telling you. Read it over again, and believe in God's Holy Word. To believe in His Word is to practice it! You have become new, and old things and ways must pass away as you grow in Christ.

Now that you are a new person and are actively walking in the Spirit, it is time to perfect your swagger, charisma, and charm to present the beautiful you. Carry yourself as a representative of Christ. Your walk should be toward the Gospel. Your charisma is your leadership, guiding your brothers and sisters to Christ. Your charm is your gentle guidance from the fruit of the Spirit. In all that you say or do, it should be for the glory of God (1 Corinthians 10:31). Remember, you are the light of the world!

Examine Yourself

> Examine yourselves whether ye be in the faith; prove
> your own selves. Know ye not your own selves, how
> that Jesus Christ is in you, except ye be reprobates?
> —2 Corinthians 13:5

> Wherefore gird up the loins of your mind, be sober,
> and hope to the end for the grace that is to be brought
> unto you at the revelation of Jesus Christ.
> —1 Peter 1:13

As I read the scripture, suggesting to examine myself, I think of Jesus when He stooped down and began to write on the ground, not answering the scribes and Pharisees who wanted to stone a woman accused of adultery. When Jesus finished writing, He stood up and said, "He that is without sin among you let him first cast a stone at her" (John 8:7). Jesus was telling everyone to examine him or herself to ponder honestly if they were in the faith by looking back over their life to determine if he or she were sin free. God has asked us not to judge one another. How can we judge someone when we all have sinned and have fallen short of the glory of God because we are born into sin? Do not be like a hypocrite casting out the mote in someone else's eye before examining yourself and removing the beam from your own eye (Matthew 7:5).

I can easily say to you, think back over your life to determine if you are sin free. However, that is something that I will not say. I can only show you the questions that I have asked myself in my self-examination. I asked myself, why go back? I went back to ask God to forgive me for all my past sins and the sins that I may not remember. I understand that I was born into sin; however, I am reborn, and I should think of today and each day in the present and examine myself daily and examine my future plans to determine if they are in the faith and the will of God. I ask myself, is there anything that I have thought about doing or saying that I know I should not do or say? Am I doing God's will, or am I taking matters into my own hands? Am I behaving as though Jesus is with me and the Holy Spirit abides within me? Am I able to recognize when the adversary is tempting me? Have I truly turned my life over to Christ, or am I playing a Christian game of being holy on Sunday only? Do I love my neighbor as I love myself?

Examine yourself by asking the difficult questions that only you can answer.

Written Examination

1. Who is God?
   _____

2. Who is Jesus Christ, and why did He die for us?
   _____

3. List the three Spirits in the Trinity.
   _____

4. What is an example of God's glory?
   _____

5. What is salvation, and what should you do to receive it?
   _____

6. What is baptism? Explain the symbolism of baptism.
   _____
   _____
   _____

7. Explain the essence of your soul, your body, and your spirit.
   _____
   _____
   _____

8. Name the fruit of the Spirit.
   _____

9. Located in the scripture John 14:26, who is the Comforter?

10. Explain faith using the scripture found in Hebrews 11:1.

11. Name nine gifts of the Spirit.

12. Explain the temple, and notate with scripture.

13. List five different types of prayers.

14. List the symbolic and spiritual components of the full armor of God and why you should wear the armor.

15. Who is the adversary? Notate a scripture that tells you how to make him flee.

16. Who are the Creators?

17. Why should you become beautiful for Christ?

18. How do you let your light shine?
_____
_____

19. What is internalization, and how do you apply it to the Scripture?
_____
_____
_____

20. Internalize Proverbs 3:5–6.
_____
_____
_____

21. Do you believe Jesus Christ is the Son of God who was crucified and died for the redemptions of our sins, was buried, and rose on the third day, and is seated at the right hand of Father God in heaven?
_____

22. Do you love the Lord God with all your heart, soul, and might?
_____

23. Locate in the Holy Bible a description of heaven, and describe it.
_____
_____
_____

24. What qualities does God seek in us when we worship Him, and why?
_____
_____

An answer key to the written examination is intentionally omitted to initiate diligence with your studies and dialogue with your pastor or Sunday school teacher.

Beautiful for Christ!

Celebrate your walk by worshipping the Lord in the beauty of holiness.

May the Almighty God continue to bless you richly and keep His loving arms around you so that you may bring joy unto God and the angels of God in heaven, now and forever. For this is my prayer, in Jesus's name I pray. Amen.

About the Author

Deaconess LaDwyina Tolar-Slater's love and respect for God have proven to be extremely important, leading her to accept one of her many callings from God: to serve others with spiritual purpose. Deaconess Slater is a graduate of Roosevelt University and Worsham College of Mortuary Science. Soon after receiving her licenses as a funeral director and embalmer, LaDwyina founded Westgate Funerals and Tributes and began serving and comforting the hearts of many bereaved families for more than thirty years until her retirement in 2018. In her own words, she explained the reason for her calling: "I was called to serve and comfort bereaved families by reminding them that God's love is real and everlasting."

Deaconess Slater's professionalism did not go unrecognized; she received the Most Influential African American Business Leadership Award in 2017, and she is also the recipient of the Leading Lady of Lake County Award. You can also find her listed in the American Directory of Who's Who in Executives and Businesses, located in the Library of Congress.

In her free time, LaDwyina enjoys sharing God's Holy Word with her husband Deacon Gregory Slater, her family and friends. She also loves reading and listening to Gospel music. Deaconess Slater's most recent calling was a vivid vision from God inspiring her to write Beautiful for Christ.

This magnificent leading lady and woman of God obeyed God's command and is sharing her vision with you and the world.

CPSIA information can be obtained
at www.ICGtesting.com
Printed in the USA
LVHW041752160223
739686LV00003B/266